MITZIE WILSON
BARBECUE RECIPES

HAMLYN

Produced by New Leaf Productions

Photography by Mick Duff
Design by Jim Wire
Series Editor: Elizabeth Gibson
Typeset by System Graphics

First published in 1985 by
Hamlyn Publishing
Bridge House, 69 London Road
Twickenham, Middlesex, England

ISBN 0 600 32496 6

Printed in Spain

Larsa D. L. TF. 556 – 1985

NOTE

1. Metric and imperial measurements have been calculated separately. Use one set of measurements only as they are not exact equivalents.

2. All spoon measures are level unless otherwise stated.

We would like to thank:
Redring Electric Ltd., Peterborough, for the use of their electric barbecue. Dickens and Jones, Regent Street, London W1. for the loan of Guzzini acrylic and melamine table ware, Bodum cutlery, Boda glassware and Södahl table napkins and place mats. Cloud 9 Designs for a selection of paper plates, napkins and octagonal shape plastic ware. Special thanks to Julie Bessens, Alison Graham, Jackie Lambert and Nichola Langley, Home Economics students from the Polytechnic of North London, for their assistance during photography. Denise Clarke for typing the manuscript.

CONTENTS

INTRODUCTION

Everybody loves giving or going to a barbecue. Is it the smoky flavour that finds its way into the food, the crisp, slightly burnt coating, or the tender succulence of the barbecue food that is so tempting? Is it the warmth of the coals to huddle around, the freshness of outdoors, the gathering of family and friends, or just the fun of the cooking? Whatever the reason, there is definitely something about barbecue food that we cannot resist.

Cooking over an open fire was of course the only way in ancient times; but with the development of spits, clay ovens, fire places and eventually enclosed cooking stoves we became more sophisticated, forgot traditions and lost the delights of open-fire cooking. That need no longer be true, however, for nowadays we can buy barbecues from the most simple to the most sophisticated and efficient; in confidence we can cook a wide range of recipes to perfection—outdoors!

Why is it, then, that many cooks stick to beefburgers, steaks, chicken portions or plain chops? They're certainly quick and always tasty, but why not use the barbecue to its full advantage, as you would a normal cooker? If you're planning an everyday meal, why not consider cooking it on the barbecue? Unless there's a downpour of rain, there's absolutely no reason not to cook on a barbecue throughout most of the year.

This book aims to give you instructions for choosing and cooking all the basic meats, fish and poultry together with interesting and unusual recipes to make your barbecue food particularly delicious. Barbecueing needn't be limited only to meats or fish; there are recipes for vegetables and fruits, too. Together with relishes, sauces, salads, and hot breads, these recipes will make your barbecue meal complete.

WHICH BARBECUE?

There is such a bewildering choice of barbecues on sale that it can be difficult to decide which one to buy. Basically they fall into five categories.

The Brazier is the most basic design of barbecue. It is simply a circular firebox with a grill-rack over the top. Look for one which has an easily adjustable grill-rack so that you can move the food nearer or further away from the fire. Look too for sturdy legs or wheels so that you can move or store the barbecue,

and check that it is a convenient height for you. If possible buy one with a hood or windshield to deter cool breezes and to help prevent swirling smoke. A small shelf or work surface attached is useful for resting food, seasonings and equipment. Some braziers with a hood may also have supports for a spit attachment, which rotates by battery or electric motor.

The Hibachi has become popular because it is so inexpensive and convenient for carrying. Hibachis are simple and efficient. They consist of a cast iron grate with vents that allow the passage of air over the coals to make them burn hotter and more evenly. The Hibachi can be round, square or oblong, with either single, double or even triple grates. Many of them fold in half for easy carrying. Brackets at the back of the Hibachi allow the grill-racks to be lowered or raised. The Hibachi is ideal for picnic or beach barbecues or for those wanting to take a barbecue with them on a camping or caravanning holiday.

Kettle Grills have the advantage of a vented hood or domed cover. When closed, this helps to speed up the cooking by sealing in the heat, as does an oven; it also intensifies the smoky flavour. When open, the hood acts as a good windshield. Kettle grills are more expensive, but they are usually large with attached trays, work surfaces and tool racks. Kettle grills are excellent for cooking large joints of meat, whole chickens—and even turkeys—since when closed the grill can be left unattended for some time. The deep fire-bowl should always have an easily adjustable vent to control the air flow to the coals.

Rotisserie Grills are sometimes known as wagon grills since they are usually large rectangular boxes mounted on a wheeled trolley with a spit roast, chopping boards, shelves, trays and tool racks attached. Levers at the front of the grill allow the rack to be lowered or raised, and the spit rod or rotisserie is supported across the grill by brackets at either side, which can also be adjusted. The spit is usually battery or electrically operated. Because of their size and weight these grills are generally confined to patio use. They are not easy to move, dismantle or store.

Gas and Electric Barbecues use natural lava rock which is heated by a gas flame (from bottled gas) or an electric element. They emit a radiant heat that is adjustable so food can be cooked accurately, with all the flavour you'd expect from barbecueing. The lava rock lasts for years, so there's no ash to clear up. After the food is cooked, the rock can be cleaned by covering the grill with foil and turning up the heat until the grease and deposits burn off. When the lava rocks have cooled, a lid conveniently encloses the entire barbecue.

MAKING THE FIRE

Situate the barbecue in a convenient place, not too far from the kitchen, not too near trees, hedges or dry grass. It is worth lining the fire bed with a double thickness of foil; this reflects the heat towards the food, helps protect the barbecue itself and makes cleaning easy. (Just gather up the ash in the foil and throw away.) If the barbecue does not have air vents, it is worth placing a layer of gravel or manufactured fire base in the fire bed to improve air circulation. Pour the charcoal into the fire bed to a depth of 5cm/2in—it should not be too tightly packed—leaving plenty of gaps to allow the air to circulate. Then pile a small pyramid of coals in the centre of the bed.

FIRE LIGHTERS

It takes time to get the coals to the right temperature for cooking, anything from 20 minutes to 1 hour, so you may need a fire starter. Once the coals become hot enough, they will be covered in a coat of ash. Spread the coals evenly over the fire bed and place the grill-rack over the coals to begin cooking.

Solid and granulated fire starters: Crumble two or three pieces of solid white fire lighter blocks amongst the pyramid of coals, or sprinkle on the granules. Ignite with a match or taper at several points and leave until the coals are ready for cooking, i.e. after about 25–35 minutes, when they will be covered in grey ash.

Liquid fire starter: Follow the manufacturers' instructions carefully. The liquid is poured onto cold briquets and allowed to soak in before lighting with a long match or taper.

Jellied Alcohol or 'canned heat': Place two or three teaspoonfuls of this jelly amongst the coals before igniting. (Take care to make sure the jelly container is stored well away from the heat.)

Electric fire starters: Portable electric starter elements can be bought which are simply placed near the base of the coals and after 5 or 10 minutes the coals will begin to burn. Some expensive barbecues will have their own built-in electric fire starters.

> NEVER USE PETROL, PARAFFIN, METHYLATED SPIRITS or LIGHTER FUEL.
> They are dangerous and leave a nasty taste in the food.

TO CONTROL THE FIRE

Open all the air vents to increase the temperature of the fire, and close them partially to reduce it. Push the coals tightly together where you need most heat, or spread them apart for less concentrated heat. Tap the coals occasionally and turn them to expose more heat. If you want to cook for long periods of time, keep a rim of coals warming up around the fire to move into place as the other coals turn to ash. Adding new cold coals will just cool down the fire. Dampen flames or flare-ups with a small spray of water. Flames burn and char food rather than cooking it.

TO PUT OUT THE FIRE

Put out the fire when you've finished cooking so that you can save the coals for next time. Put the lid down over the barbecue and close air vents, or place the coals in a metal bucket and cover with a metal lid.

CARE OF YOUR BARBECUE

Line the firebox with foil before cooking, whenever possible. Always keep metal barbecues covered when not in use; a sheet of plastic tied around will do. They will rust if left out in the rain. Soak grill-racks in hot, soapy water; dry well and store inside; oil grill-racks again before use.

GENERAL COOKING HINTS

1. For most grilling, position the grill rack about 5–8cm/2–3in above the hot coals. If the food burns too quickly, move the grill rack further away. If the coals have died down and the food cooks too slowly, lower the rack towards coals and turn the coals occasionally. Cooking times are difficult to estimate since the wind and air temperature both affect the fire, but with experience you will soon be able to gauge cooking times and alter the fire accordingly. The cooking times suggested in this book are only guidelines. Remember to allow 20 minutes to 1 hour for the coals to get really hot before cooking.
2. Keep a fine water spray or mister handy to dampen any flames caused by dripping fat.
3. Remember that you are cooking on a flat grill, and choose food of even thickness—as flat as possible—not too thick, or it will burn on the outside before the centre is cooked.
4. Always buy the best possible cuts of meat since barbecue cooking is too fast to tenderise meat.
5. Marinate meat, poultry and fish to help tenderise and add flavour.
6. Fresh or frozen meat will cook quicker when brought up to room temperature beforehand.
7. Score the fat around steaks or chops before cooking to prevent the meat from curling up.
8. Brush the barbecue grill rack with oil to prevent food from sticking.

9. Cook delicate foods such as fish, burgers or sliced vegetables in hinged wire baskets so that they can be turned easily, or cover the grill-rack with foil.

10. Add a few sprigs of fresh herbs such as rosemary, thyme or marjoram, or a few cloves of garlic to the hot coals towards the end of cooking, to create subtle and aromatic flavours.

11. For genuine smoky flavours, buy hickory or juniper wood chips, specially prepared for barbecues, and add to the coals for the last 10 minutes' cooking.

TOOLS

Tongs and forks are essential items for turning and picking up hot, barbecued food. Buy long wooden-handled ones, so that you don't scorch your hands.

Brushes: Use a pure bristle brush (not plastic!) for basting food with fat or marinades; again, but one with a long wooden handle.

Foil: Not just for lining the fire bed, or for wrapping food before cooking, but also for wrapping around delicate food such as fish tails and chicken wings, which may char. A double layer of foil also makes a hotplate for cooking bacon, burgers, or even eggs. Prick the foil with a skewer when cooking greasy foods such as hamburgers. Foil is also useful for making trays to catch dripping fat and juices when spit roasting.

Oven gloves and aprons are absolutely essential, as barbecueing can be fiercely hot and very dirty!

Pans: Keep one or two small cast-iron or heavy-based pans for heating sauces on the barbecue. The pans will become blackened with use. Choose long-handled pans if possible as the handles will get hot!

Skewers: Keep a variety of long and short metal skewers for kebabs, and for testing cooked meats. Wooden skewers are useful too; you can cover exposed ends with foil if they begin to burn.

Water spray or sprinkler: Useful for dousing flames.

Hinged baskets: A variety of baskets is available; choose a large, flat, hinged basket for cooking sliced vegetables, burgers, thinly sliced meat or bacon. These foods will then be secure and are much easier to turn. Fish-shaped, concave, baskets in various shapes and sizes are particularly useful for delicate fish, which can otherwise be difficult to turn during cooking.

Meat thermometers are very useful for determining the internal cooked temperature of the meat, especially when spit roasting.

Wire brush: for cleaning and brushing off grease and food from the grill-racks.

WHICH FUEL?

Charcoal is the most widely used fuel—also very messy.

Lumpwood charcoal is made by charring hardwood in a kiln. The lumps are graded by size. It is easy to ignite but can give off sparks. It burns quite quickly and leaves a lot of ash. The coals give off carbon monoxide gas so **never** cook with it in a closed room.

Charcoal Briquets are made from compressed hardwood and come in neat, uniform nuggets. They take several minutes of intense heat to ignite, so use firelighters or a commercial ignition agent to get the fire going see page 6. **(Never use petrol, lighter fluid or meths.)** Briquets burn for a long time with little smoke or odour. They glow rather than flame, and in daylight you may not see the glow—just a fine grey ash that appears as the fire spreads.

Charbar: A relatively new product which seals charcoal into cardboard trays rather like egg boxes. This saves the dust and dirt and the cardboard is impregnated with a lighting agent for ease of use.

SPIT ROASTING

A traditional method of roasting meat, this is a delicious way of cooking succulent joints of beef, pork or boned stuffed lamb, as well as chickens.

Choose meat that is boned, rolled and secured tightly with string. The meat must be evenly shaped so that it will balance on the spit and turn evenly. Pass the spit through the centre of the food and grip it on either side with the spit forks. Hold the spit between both hands and check the balance; the food should roll without suddenly dropping to one side. Check during cooking and tighten the grip on the meat or alter the balance if necessary.

Make a drip pan from a double thickness of foil. It should be exactly the same size as the food and at least 4cm/1½in deep. Clear the hot coals from the fire bed and place the drip tray directly under the spit. Build the coals up around either side and cook for the time recommended in the recipe.

SPIT-ROASTED SIRLOIN
Serves 8

Worth cooking, especially if you like your beef rare.

1.5–2kg/3–4lb sirloin of beef, boned and rolled
2 tablespoons oil
2 teaspoons French mustard
2 teaspoons Worcestershire sauce

Insert the rotisserie spit carefully through the centre of the meat, checking that it is well balanced. Mix the oil, mustard and Worcestershire sauce together and brush over the joint. Cook over hot coals for 1–1¼ hours, basting frequently. To test when cooked, insert a skewer into the centre of the joint; the juices should run pink but not too bloody for rare meat. For well done meat cook for 1 hour then cover with foil. Cook for a further 1 hour; uncover and cook for a further 15–20 minutes. If you have a meat thermometer, the internal temperature should read 130°F for rare meat, 170°F for well-done meat.

SPIT-ROASTED SPARERIBS
Serves 4–6

A whole rack of ribs is easy to cook on a spit and the meat stays moist and juicy. Ask your butcher for an American style rack of ribs.

1 small rack of pork ribs
1 quantity Spicy barbecue sauce (p.56)

Trim the spareribs of any excess fat. Thread the spit rod through the meat between every second pair of ribs. Secure at either end with the spit forks, and make sure it is evenly balanced. Spit roast the ribs over hot coals for 20 minutes; then, using a long-handled brush, coat the ribs with barbecue sauce. Brush every 10 minutes or so until the meat is cooked after another 30–40 minutes. When cooked the meat will be crisp on the outside but tender between the bones. Carve the meat into individual ribs and serve with any remaining barbecue sauce.

KENTUCKY SPIT-ROASTED CHICKEN
Serves 4

Roast chicken cooked on a spit has a succulent smoky flavour. Try this delicious spicy, sweet coating on chicken drumsticks too.

1 lemon
1.5kg/3lb oven-ready chicken
pinch grated nutmeg
½ teaspoon celery salt
1 teaspoon paprika
½ teaspoon salt
1 tablespoon brown sugar
black pepper
50g/2oz butter, melted

Cut the lemon in half. Place one half inside the chicken with a sprinkling of salt and pepper. Truss the chicken tightly. Place the rotisserie spit through the chicken and tie the chicken legs tightly together around the spit. Squeeze the juice from the remaining lemon and mix with the spices, sugar and butter. Spit roast chicken over hot coals for 1–1½ hours, brushing frequently with the spices and basting with the juices from the drip pan. Pierce the chicken with a skewer; if cooked the juices will run clear.

APRICOT AND ROSEMARY SPIT-ROASTED LEG OF LAMB
Serves 8

Ask the butcher to bone the lamb for you, or using a small sharp knife, scrape the flesh away, following the bone down as far as you can. Cut through the join and remove bone.

1 small onion
1 tablespoon oil
3 sprigs fresh rosemary (or 1 teaspoon dried)
50g/2oz fresh breadcrumbs
397-g/14-oz can apricot halves in natural juices
one 2-kg/4-lb leg of lamb, boned

Peel and very finely chop the onion. Heat the oil in a small pan and fry onion until transparent. Chop the rosemary and add to the onion with the breadcrumbs; stir well. Drain the apricot halves, reserving the juice. Chop half of the fruit and reserve remainder for decoration. Add the chopped fruit to the breadcrumbs with enough apricot juice to make a soft stuffing; season with salt and pepper and place stuffing in the centre of the lamb. Tie lamb in a neat shape with string and secure ends with cocktail sticks making sure it is tight, or it will lose its shape. Mix oil with remaining apricot juices and brush over the joint. Attach the rotisserie spit and cook over hot coals for about 1½ hours, brushing with the apricot syrup. Serve garnished with the apricot halves.

CHICKEN

Chicken benefits from cooking over charcoal as it picks up a delectable smoky flavour, but you must take care not to overcook or dry out the chicken. Too much heat and the skin will burn, so always grill about 10cm/4in above the coals. Too little heat and the chicken will dry out.

Whole birds are best flattened out—this is quite simple. Place the chicken on its breast and, using poultry shears, cut along the length of the backbone. (If you don't have poultry shears, insert a knife inside the bird, along the backbone, and cut firmly down along the backbone.) Open the bird out as much as possible, place it on a board breast side up, and firmly strike the bird down on the breastbone to break it. Smash down the centre to break the wishbone and ribs; then open out the bird.

To flavour the chicken: Spread garlic and herb butter under the skin or place thin slices of lemon, bacon or sprigs of herb under the skin before cooking.

To cook whole chicken: Grill about 10cm/4in over hot coals. Grill bone side down for three quarters of the cooking time so as not to char the skin, then turn over and cook skin side down. Brush bird frequently with oil and melted butter or marinade (see pages 54–57). Sprinkle with salt, pepper and herbs. A whole 1.5-kg/3½-lb bird will take about 40–50 minutes to cook. To test when cooked, press the chicken breast or thigh with a finger; it should feel firm, not spongy, and the juices will run clear when the chicken is pierced with a skewer.

CHICKEN PORTIONS

These are ideal for barbecueing; you can add so many coatings and flavourings before cooking to make a wide range of delicious recipes. Chicken is best cooked on the bone to prevent it from drying out. Large wing or leg portions will take about 25–35 minutes to cook. Single legs or wing joints will take about 15–20 minutes to cook.

SOME QUICK AND SIMPLE GLAZES FOR CHICKEN

Sweet and Sour: Mix 3 tablespoons clear honey with 2 teaspoons Worcestershire sauce, 1 tablespoon soy sauce and 1 tablespoon tomato ketchup. Brush over chicken joints and grill.

Marmalade and Ginger: Mix 3 tablespoons coarse-cut orange marmalade with a pinch of ginger and 1 tablespoon soy or Worcestershire sauce. Brush over chicken and grill.

Mango and Chilli: Mix 4 tablespoons mango chutney with 2 teaspoons hot chilli sauce. Brush over chicken and grill.

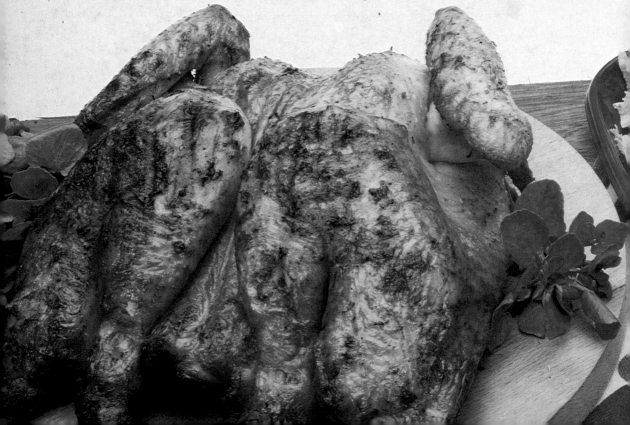

SESAME CHICKEN
Serves 6–8

Cut down the quantity of garlic if you like—but you will be surprised how this quantity imparts a delicious flavour and wonderful aroma without being overpowering.

two 1.25–1.5–kg/2½–3–lb chickens, quartered
4 cloves garlic, chopped finely
juice of 1 lemon
2 teaspoons ginger
250ml/8fl oz cooking oil
40g/1½oz sesame seeds
125ml/4fl oz soy sauce

Place chicken in casserole dish. Mix all other ingredients and pour over chicken. Marinate 30 minutes at least. Cut 8 pieces of foil in large squares. Top each with chicken and 1 tablespoon marinade. Wrap tightly. Barbecue 40–50 minutes on grill. When done unwrap; add extra marinade to each piece of chicken; put back on grill until seeds are golden. Serve immediately.

MINT-STUFFED CHICKEN PORTIONS
Serves 4

Use bottled mint sauce to flavour this fresh-tasting, lemony chicken recipe.

4 slices bread
1 lemon
2 teaspoons mint sauce
4 chicken joints
50g/2oz butter, melted
2 tablespoons oil

Roughly break the bread; place in a bowl. Coarsely grate lemon rind and squeeze juice; add with mint sauce. Mash together with a fork. Lift the skin from the breast part of the chicken and pack stuffing under the skin. Grill bone side down, over hot coals for about 15 minutes. Brush with oil and butter. Turn over and grill for a further 10 minutes. Turn occasionally to brush with butter and oil.

GOLDEN TANDOORI CHICKEN
Serves 8

The traditional orange colour of tandoori comes from food colouring. If you want to use it, just paint red or orange food colouring over the chicken before marinating. Use a commercial blend of tandoori spice if you do not have all the different spices.

8 small chicken portions
3 tablespoons lemon juice
1 teaspoon salt
425ml/15fl oz natural yogurt
½ onion, finely chopped
1 clove garlic, crushed
1 teaspoon fresh ginger, grated
½ teaspoon ground cardamom
½ teaspoon cinnamon
pinch of ground cloves
good pinch of black pepper
pinch of ground nutmeg
2 teaspoons garam masala
OR tandoori spice

Place the chicken in one or two large casserole dishes. Sprinkle both sides with lemon juice and salt. Leave for 20–30 minutes. Brush the chicken with food colouring if liked. Mix together the yogurt, onion, garlic and spices or garam masala. Pour over the chicken making sure it is coated on all sides, cover and refrigerate for at least 6, or up to 24 hours. Take the chicken out of the marinade, shaking off as much marinade as possible. Grill chicken bone side down over hot coals for 20 minutes. Turn over and cook for a further 10–15 minutes until tender.

YAKITORI—JAPANESE CHICKEN
Makes 4 kebabs

The strong flavour of soy sauce goes well with barbecued food.

350g/12oz boned chicken breast
100g/4oz button mushrooms
4 spring onions, cut into 2.5-cm/1-in lengths
4 tablespoons Japanese soy sauce
3 tablespoons medium sherry
pinch of ground ginger
2 teaspoons soft brown sugar

Cut the chicken into 2.5-cm/1-in cubes and thread onto wooden or metal skewers with the mushrooms and spring onions. Mix together the remaining ingredients and brush over the kebabs. Grill over hot coals, basting frequently with marinade for 10–12 minutes. Remove the meat from the skewers and place on top of bowls of plain boiled rice. Decorate with spring onion brushes. (Cut spring onions into 7.5cm/3in lengths, shred the ends finely with a sharp knife and leave in iced water until the ends curl up).

CARIBBEAN CHICKEN THIGHS
Serves 6

Chicken thighs are an economical buy, and quite meaty. Grill them just brushed with butter and oil, or soak in this marinade to make the meat tender and tangy.

6 chicken thigh pieces
1 tablespoon dark rum
1 tablespoon soy sauce
1 small can pineapple rings in natural juices
salt and black pepper
4 tablespoons oil

Make two slits on each side of the chicken thighs. Mix rum, soy and pineapple juice together, brush over chicken and leave for 2 hours. Season lightly with salt and pepper, and grill over hot coals for 15–20 minutes, brushing with oil and turning the chicken frequently. Grill pineapple rings for a 2–3 minutes on each side and serve with chicken.

CHICKEN TIKKA
Serves 6

Another version of tandoori. It is traditionally cooked in a clay oven, but cooked over barbecue coals they have an even more interesting flavour.

3 chicken breasts, boned
1 teaspoon salt
4 tablespoons lemon juice
2.5-cm/1-in piece fresh root ginger
2 cloves garlic
150ml/¼ pint natural yogurt
1 teaspoon ground cumin
pinch of hot curry powder
pinch of cayenne
orange food colouring, optional
100g/4oz butter, melted

Remove skin from chicken and cut into 2.5-cm/1-in cubes. Thread loosely onto wooden or metal skewers. Sprinkle each with salt and lemon juice. Leave for 15–20 minutes. Peel and grate the ginger and crush the garlic; add to the yogurt with the spices and food colouring. Brush this mixture all over the chicken. Cover and leave to marinate for several hours, overnight if possible. Grill over hot coals, brushing with melted butter for 10–15 minutes, turning frequently. Serve with wedges of lemon, sliced onion rings and cucumber.

MARYLAND KEBABS
Makes 4

Choose a small corn on the cob—or preferably buy the baby corns; they look and taste wonderful, and don't have to be cooked first.

1 corn cob, or baby corns, frozen or canned
2 bananas
1 tablespoon lemon juice
8 rashers smoked streaky bacon, rinds removed
2 large chicken breasts
salt and pepper
50g/2oz melted butter
1 tablespoon honey

Remove husks from corn and cook cob in boiling water for 6–10 minutes until the kernels are tender. Drain. Using a serated knife, cut the corn into 1-cm/½-in thick slices. Peel bananas and cut into 2.5-cm/1-in lengths. Dip in lemon juice and wrap half a rasher of bacon around each piece. Skin chicken and cut breast into 2.5-cm/1-in pieces. Thread corn, bananas, bacon rolls and chicken together on metal skewers. Sprinkle with a little salt and pepper and brush with melted butter and honey. Grill over hot coals for 8–10 minutes. Turn and frequently brush with butter and honey.

POUSSIN WITH LEMON–BUTTER BASTE

Serves 6

Buy young poussin or spring chickens, fresh or frozen from a butcher or supermarket. Serve half a bird per person.

3 poussin
6 sprigs fresh tarragon OR rosemary
1 lemon, sliced
75g/3oz butter, softened
salt and pepper
4 tablespoons sunflower or corn oil

Cut the poussin in half using poultry shears (see page 10.) Open the chicken out and flatten the breast bone. Lift the chicken skin away from the breast and spread softened butter under the skin. Place 2 lemon slices and 2 sprigs of fresh herb in each. Sprinkle birds with salt and pepper. Brush with oil. Grill over hot coals for 10–15 minutes on each side, brushing well with oil, until the flesh is firm and the skin crisp.

BARBECUED CHICKEN DRUMSTICKS

Serves 10

Drumsticks are economical for large barbecue parties; buy them in bulk from the freezer centre and thaw overnight in the fridge.

4 tablespoons tomato ketchup
4 tablespoons brown fruity sauce
1 tablespoon malt vinegar
1 tablespoon black treacle
10 chicken drumsticks

Mix the ketchup, fruity sauce, vinegar and treacle together in a small bowl. Brush each drumstick with the glaze and grill over hot coals for 15–20 minutes. Turn chicken frequently and brush with the glaze. Serve with fried onions and hot bread, or crisps.

DUCK, TURKEY & RABBIT

CHINESE ORANGE DUCK
Serves 4

Use poultry shears or ask the butcher to cut the duck into quarters. The duck should be well cooked until the skin is crisp—delicious with the sticky sweet sauce.

4 spring onions
pinch of ginger
1 teaspoon turmeric
2 tablespoons dark soy sauce
4 tablespoons orange marmalade
salt and black pepper
one 2–2.5-kg/4–5-lb duck, quartered
1 orange

Trim and finely chop the spring onions, placing them in a large shallow dish with the ginger, turmeric, soy and marmalade; mix well together. Season the duck with salt and pepper, add to the dish and brush the sauce all over the duck until well coated. Cover and leave for 4 hours. Place the grill about 10cm/4in above medium-hot coals and cook the duck, bone side down, for 15 minutes. Turn duck over and brush with the sauce. Cook for a further 10–15 minutes, taking care not to burn the skin. Turn over again and cook for a further 15–20 minutes or until the flesh feels firm. Turn duck over and crispen the skin for the last 5–10 minutes. Slice the orange, brush with marinade and grill for 5 minutes. Serve with Chinese leaves (cabbage.)

SPICED TURKEY SLICES
Serves 6

Turkey escalopes can be found in many supermarkets and butchers; but if you have any trouble finding them, buy turkey breast and prepare it by placing it between damp greaseproof paper and flattening it with a rolling pin. Chicken can also be cooked this way. Marinate the poultry, or it will dry out.

4 tablespoons olive oil
¼ teaspoon chilli pepper
pinch of ground mace
pinch of ground cardamom
pinch of salt
½ teaspoon freshly ground black pepper
6 turkey escalopes

Mix all the marinade ingredients together and pour into a large shallow dish. Add the turkey escalopes and turn to coat them with the marinade. Leave for 2 hours, turning occasionally. Place the grill about 10–15cm/4–6in above medium-hot coals. Grill turkey for 5 minutes, turning and frequently brushing with the marinade, until firm and golden. Take care not to overcook. Serve with slices of green pepper.

RABBIT WITH MUSTARD
Serves 4

Ask your butcher to joint the rabbit for you, or use poultry shears. The meat can be dry so baste it frequently with this not-too-hot mustard glaze.

1 rabbit, cut into 6 joints
salt and pepper
50g/2oz butter
2 tablespoons oil
1 bay leaf
1 tablespoon fresh thyme, chopped
2 tablespoons coarse-grain mustard

Sprinkle rabbit with salt and pepper. Place the remaining ingredients in a small pan. Grill rabbit over medium hot coals and place the pan of sauce on the grill. Turn and brush the rabbit with the sauce frequently. Grill for about 30 minutes or until the flesh feels firm and the juices run clear when the meat is pierced with a skewer. Serve with grilled apple rings.

PORK

Lean pork grills to perfection over barbecue coals—providing you cook it with care. Pork must be cooked thoroughly and so needs long cooking over *medium-hot* coals. (Don't cook over very hot coals or the meat will burn.) Choose lean cuts such as chops and loin of pork. It is always best to marinate pork (try the Oil marinade page 54) to add flavour and to prevent it from drying out, but brush with oil and flavourings during cooking, too. Belly pork can be rather fatty and cause flames, so choose the lean thick pieces. Cubed pork is also ideal for kebabs.

PORK CHOPS

Choose thick-cut pork chops. Loin chops are the best choice. Trim them of excess fat, or it will drip onto the fire and flare up. Brush the chops with oil and season (or marinade if preferred). Grill over very hot coals to sear the surface, for about 2–3 minutes each side, then move to less hot coals to continue cooking for a further 6 minutes on each side.

Bay and Orange Glaze: Mix the grated rind and juice of 1 orange with 1 tablespoon oil, 1 teaspoon ground dried bay leaves and a good shake of salt and pepper. Brush over chops and grill.

Apple-Topped Chops: Core crisp dessert apples and cut into thick rings. Brush each slice with lemon juice and honey. Grill over warm coals for 1 minute on each side. Place over grilled chops, brush with a little more honey and grill for a further 2–3 minutes.

BLUE CHEESE CHOPS
For 6 chops

Blue cheese and tender pork make a wonderful combination. Use mild or strong blue cheese according to taste.

6 pork chops
4 tablespoons olive oil
100-g/4-oz Danish Blue or Roquefort cheese
25g/1oz walnut pieces
fresh basil, chopped

Brush the pork chops with olive oil and sprinkle with salt and pepper. Grill chops over hot coals for about 7 minutes on each side, or until the juices run clear when meat is pierced with a skewer. When chops are brown and crisp, place a thin slice of cheese on top of each; sprinkle with a few walnut pieces and cook for a further 2–3 minutes or until the cheese melts. Serve sprinkled with a little fresh basil.

CHILLI PORK
Serves 6

Thin, boned chump chops marinated in this pungent mixture are delicious.

1 small green pepper
2 small green chillies
1 clove garlic
4 tomatoes
1 small onion
4 tablespoons medium-sweet white wine
salt and black pepper
6 boned chump chops

Cut the green pepper and chillies in half, discarding core and seeds. (Do not touch face or eyes with your fingers as the chilli juice burns.) Peel garlic. Skin and deseed tomatoes. Peel onion. Place all vegetables, wine and a good shake of salt and pepper into a food processor or liquidiser and blend to a paste. Place chops in a shallow dish and spread with the pepper mixture, cover and leave for 2 hours. Remove meat and drain off marinade and heat in a small pan, Sear the chops over hot coals for 3–4 minutes on each side. Move to warm coals and cook for a further 10–12 minutes, or until the meat is firm and golden brown. Serve each chop with a little of the marinade.

PORK CHOPS WITH CAPER AND GHERKIN MARINADE
Serves 4

Sparerib chops are quite meaty, and capers and gherkins make them piquant. Serve any remaining marinade with the meat.

4 sparerib chops
2 tablespoons capers
2 gherkins, chopped
4 tablespoons dry white wine or cider
2 teaspoons sugar
2 tablespoons olive, sunflower or soya oil
½ teaspoon mustard

Place the sparerib chops in a large, shallow dish with the bay leaf. Scatter the capers and gherkins over the top. Mix wine, sugar oil and mustard and pour over. Leave for 2 hours to marinate. Drain chops and grill over hot coals for 6–7 minutes on each side. Move chops to warm coals and continue cooking for a further 10–15 minutes, basting frequently with the marinade. Cook until the juices run clear when meat is pierced with a skewer. Serve with grilled onion rings.

GREEK SOUVLAKI

Serves 8

If you do not have all the spices for this recipe use 2 teaspoons garam masala instead (from Indian stores). Use Greek Retsina or Domestica wine and drink the remaining with the meal for a truly Greek flavour.

1kg/2lb boned belly pork
2 onions (one quartered)
1 clove garlic
2 bay leaves
150ml/¼ pint dry white wine
6 tablespoons oil
½ teaspoon ground cumin
½ teaspoon ground coriander
½ teaspoon cinnamon
½ teaspoon ground cardamom
salt and pepper
bay leaves

Cut the belly pork into 2.5-cm/1-in cubes. Peel and finely chop the onion and garlic. Place in a bowl with all the ingredients except the lemons; beat together and add the pork. Marinate for at least 4 hours. Thread the meat, quartered onion and bay onto skewers and grill over hot coals for 15–20 minutes, turning frequently and basting with the marinade. Serve with shredded cabbage and carrot.

SPICED BELLY PORK

These spices give a delicious, aromatic flavour to the pork. Prepare it 2 days ahead for the maximum effect.

1 tablespoon juniper berries
1 teaspoon black peppercorns
4 allspice berries
1 teaspoon dried thyme
2 bay leaves
6 tablespoons coarse-grain salt
6 thick slices belly pork

Blend the juniper, peppercorns, allspice, thyme and bay in a liquidiser or coffee grinder until coarsely ground. Stir in the salt. Coat each slice of belly pork with the spice and lay in a large glass or china dish. Cover and leave in refrigerator for 2 days. Shake off excess spices. Brush the pork with oil and grill over hot coals for 5–8 minutes on each side. Move to warm coals and cook for a further 15–20 minutes until crisp. Serve with puréed fresh tomatoes.

SWEET-AND-SOUR PORK KEBABS

Makes 8 or 9

Pork is delicious cooked with pineapple and basted with a tangy–sharp sauce.

500g/1lb lean cubed pork (fillet)
200-g/7-oz can pineapple cubes in syrup
1 green pepper
1 red pepper
1 tablespoon tomato purée
2 tablespoons brown sugar
2 tablespoons vinegar
2 teaspoons Worcestershire sauce
pinch of chilli seasoning
salt and pepper
2 teaspoons cornflour

Cut the pork into 2.5-cm/1-in pieces. Drain pineapple syrup into a small pan. Cut the peppers into 2.5-cm/1-in squares, discarding core and seeds. Thread pork, pineapple and peppers together onto metal skewers. Stir tomato purée, sugar, vinegar, Worcestershire sauce, chilli seasoning and good shake of salt and pepper into the pineapple syrup. Bring to the boil. Mix cornflour with 1 tablespoon cold water and stir into the boiling sauce. Cook for 1 minute. Brush over the kebabs. Grill kebabs over hot coals for 10–12 minutes, turning and brushing frequently with the sauce. Serve the remaining sauce separately.

DEVILLED GAMMON WITH PINEAPPLE

Use French mustard if you don't like your gammon quite so 'hot'.

**four 175-g/6-oz gammon steaks, smoked or
  unsmoked**
little melted butter
2 teaspoons English mustard
2 tablespoons demerara sugar
1 small can pineapple rings

Snip the rind around the gammon steaks to prevent them curling up. Brush each steak with melted butter, spread thickly with mustard and sprinkle with sugar. Grill over medium hot coals for 3–4 minutes on each side. Drain pineapple rings, grill for 1 minute on each side, then place on top of the gammon.

APPLE-AND-RAISIN STUFFED BACON CHOPS

Bacon chops are thickly cut, lean back-rashers. These don't take long to cook. Choose thick ones so that you can make a pocket for a sweet apple stuffing.

1 large cooking apple
knob of butter
25g/1oz raisins
oil
4 thick bacon chops

Peel and core the apple. Slice and place in a small pan with the butter. Cook over a low heat until the apples are tender. Break up with a fork and add the raisins. Using a sharp knife cut into the side of the chop to make a pocket. Do not cut all the way through the bacon. Pack the apple and raisin mixture inside the chops. Brush the chops with oil and grill over medium coals for 6–8 minutes on each side or until the meat feels firm.

SIMPLE SPARERIBS

Buy pork spareribs and not sparerib chops for true American-style ribs. Cut them into individual ribs and boil for 10 minutes before cooking to remove excess fat (or they will spit and burn). Marinate them in either the Basic or the Spicy barbecue sauces (see recipes page 56) for 1 hour. Drain and cook the ribs over hot coals for 6–8 minutes on each side. Brush well with marinade and move to cooler coals for a further 15–20 minutes, brushing frequently with the marinade until the meat is crisp but not dry.

CHINESE SPARERIBS
Serves 4 to 6

The five-spice powder makes these ribs aromatic and oriental, though it's not an essential ingredient. Look for it in Chinese shops and supermarkets.

750g/1½lb pork spareribs
5-mm/½-in piece root ginger
2 tablespoons oil
2 cloves garlic, crushed
1 green pepper
pinch of five-spice powder
1 tablespoon soy sauce
2 tablespoons dry sherry
2 tablespoons tomato purée
2 tablespoons vinegar
2 tablespoons honey

Cut the pork into individual ribs. Cook in boiling water for 10 minutes, then drain well. Peel and grate the ginger; chop the pepper, discarding core and seeds. Heat the oil in a frying pan and fry the garlic, ginger, pepper and five-spice powder together for 2–3 minutes. Add the remaining ingredients and stir well. Simmer for 5 minutes. Brush over the ribs and cook them over hot coals for 6–8 minutes on each side. Move ribs to warm coals and continue grilling for a further 20–30 minutes, brushing frequently with the marinade. Serve with rice and spring onion brushes. (See Yakitori page 13.)

LAMB

SHOULDER OF LAMB

This is the only large joint that is suitable for grilling over the coals without a spit roaster. The meat will cook crisply on the outside but be juicy pink and rare inside. Great care must be taken not to burn the outside before it is cooked through. You will need a deep charcoal fire as the lamb can take between 40 minutes and 1½ hours, and the fire must not be too hot. Spread the coals thinly if they begin to get too hot. Place the grill about 12.5cm/3in away from the coals, moving it nearer or further depending on the heat.

ROSEMARY AND GARLIC STUDDED SHOULDER

Serves 6-8

1 small shoulder of lamb
6 sprigs fresh rosemary
6 sprigs fresh thyme
4 tablespoons olive oil
3 cloves garlic, sliced
salt and black pepper

Trim excess fat from the lamb. Using a sharp knife cut two or three deep slashes right through the meat to the bone. Place a sprig of rosemary and thyme in each cut. Make small slits in the meat using just the point of a knife, and place a thin slice of garlic in each. Brush well with oil and sprinkle with salt and pepper. Grill over medium-hot coals, and turn every 10 minutes, brushing with oil. Place a few sprigs of rosemary and thyme onto the coals to give off herb-scented smoke. Test the joint after 40 minutes by pressing the thickest part of the meat. It should feel quite firm when cooked, and the juices should run clear or slightly pink, but not bloody, when the meat is pierced with a skewer. Leave the shoulder to rest for 10–15 minutes before carving. Serve with sliced sautéed courgettes and boiled new potatoes.

CHUMP CHOPS WITH PEACH AND GINGER

Serves 6

This fruity topping makes a colourful, flavourful addition to chump chops.

1 small can peach slices in natural juices
4 tablespoons dry white wine
1 teaspoon ginger
½ teaspoon dried oregano
2 tablespoons oil
1 onion, chopped
1 bay leaf
salt and black pepper
6 chump chops
1 clove garlic, optional

Drain the peach slices, reserving the juice. Place 4 tablespoons of the juice in a shallow pan with the remaining ingredients. Turn the lamb in the marinade and leave for 2 hours. Remove the lamb and dry well on kitchen paper. Cut the garlic in half and run cut surface over both sides of the chops. Grill over hot coals, for 10–15 minutes, turning and basting frequently with the marinade. The meat will feel just firm when cooked and the juices run clear when the meat is pierced. Place the peaches on top of the chops. Brush with more marinade and cook for a further 5 minutes. Serve with watercress.

LAMB CHOPS WITH GREEN PEPPERCORN AND REDCURRANT GLAZE

Serves 4

Dried green peppercorns are much milder and sweeter than black ones—delicious sprinkled on any meat. You will find them in delicatessens.

4 lean lamb chops
4 teaspoons dried green peppercorns, crushed
½ teaspoon salt
1 tablespoon oil
4 tablespoons redcurrant jelly

Trim the lamb chops of excess fat. Roughly crush the peppercorns. Mix with salt and press well onto both sides of the lamb. Brush with oil and grill the lamb over hot coals for 10 minutes on each side. Warm the redcurrant jelly and pour over both sides of the lamb just before serving.

BARBECUED LAMB RIBS
Serves 4

The breast of lamb is boiled first to remove the excess fat. Boiling also cuts down on the barbecueing time, and the sweet mustard glaze cuts through any greasiness.

1.5kg/3lb breast of lamb
2 tablespoons lemon juice
2 tablespoons soy sauce
3 tablespoons runny honey
2 tablespoons sweet vegetable chutney
1 tablespoon vinegar
2 teaspoons Worcestershire sauce
2 teaspoons French mustard
1 teaspoon tomato purée

Remove excess fat from the lamb and cut the meat into strips between the bones. Place the meat in a large saucepan. Cover with boiling water; add the lemon juice and bring to the boil. Simmer for 15 minutes; drain and allow to cool. Mix the remaining ingredients together in a small bowl and brush over the lamb. Grill over medium-hot coals for about 15–20 minutes. Turn and baste the lamb with the sauce frequently.

GREEK LAMB WITH OLIVES
Serves 8

Cooked wrapped in foil and placed on a rack just over the coals, this lamb joint will take about an hour and a half to cook until the meat begins to fall off the bone.

1-kg/2-lb half-leg or knuckle of lamb
salt and pepper
2 cloves garlic
75g/3oz butter
100g/4oz stoned black Greek olives
6 tablespoons dry white wine
4 tablespoons lemon juice
1 tablespoon chopped parsley
2 tablespoons chopped fresh mint
1 teaspoon dried oregano
1 bay leaf
salt and black pepper

Sprinkle the lamb with salt and pepper. Crush the garlic and place in a large frying pan with the butter. Heat gently until the butter melts. Add the lamb and fry it on all sides until brown. Remove from the pan and place on a large piece of foil, folding the edges up slightly. Finely chop the olives, and add to the wine with the lemon juice, parsley, mint, oregano, bay leaf and a good shake of salt and pepper. Pour mixture over the meat. Fold the foil around the lamb, securing tightly. Wrap a second piece of foil around it to prevent leakage. Place the lamb on a wire rack directly over warm coals. Cook for about 1½ hours, turning the lamb every half hour. Insert a skewer into the top of the lamb; if the juices run pink, the lamb is tender, and rare. Wait until the juices run clear if you prefer the meat well-cooked. Serve on a bed of crisp lettuce with olives and wedges of lemon.

TURKISH SHISH KEBAB
Makes 8 Kebabs

Grated onion gives this meat a savoury flavour. It's well worth marinating overnight if you can.

2 onions
125ml/¼ pint olive oil
rind and juice of 1 lemon
1 teaspoon cinnamon
½ teaspoon salt
black pepper
1kg/2lb lean shoulder of lamb, cubed
4 courgettes

Peel onions and blend in a liquidiser or food processor (or grate finely). Press onion purée through a sieve to extract juice. In a large bowl mix onion juice with the oil, lemon, cinnamon, salt and a good shake of pepper. Add the meat and turn until well coated. Cover and leave for 3–4 hours, overnight if possible. Cut away 6 long, thin strips of courgette peel, and slice the courgettes so that they look like wheels. Thread the meat and courgettes together on eight metal or wooden skewers and grill over hot coals, turning frequently for about 10 minutes. Serve with saffron rice and salad.

KIBBEH
Serves 8

Kibbeh are Lebanese minced lamb kebabs. Buy finely minced lamb and if possible mince it again (or blend in a food processor). The finer it is minced, the better the mixture will hold together. Cous-cous is a type of semolina; look for it in Continental stores.

175g/6oz finely ground cous-cous
1 small onion, peeled and grated
225g/½lb minced lamb
1½ teaspoons salt
½ teaspoon black pepper
½ teaspoon cinnamon
½ teaspoon paprika

Place the cous-cous in a large bowl, cover with cold water and leave to soak for 30 minutes. Drain, press out as much moisture as possible. Place onion in a bowl with the lamb and spices. Knead together, then knead in the cous-cous. Knead for about 10 minutes until the mixture forms a soft dough so that the mixture will not be coarse when cooked. Using damp hands divide the mixture into eight portions and roll between the palms of your hands to give long, oval, cigar-shaped sausages. Place a metal skewer onto each one and wrap the mixture tightly around it. Grill over hot coals, turning frequently for about 10 minutes. Serve with a crisp salad.

BEEF

A steak cooked to crisp sizzling succulence epitomises barbecued food, yet cooking it to that degree of perfection is not easy.

Choosing beef cuts: Steaks are ideal for grilling. Choose the best steaks—the most tender being fillet, rump, T-bone, entrecote and sirloin. If you start with a good piece of meat, the end result will be worthwhile. A tougher cut such as skirt can also be cooked, but marinate it first to tenderise. Quick-fry steaks that have been tenderised by beating are good too. Choose steak that has a marbling of fat through it, but not too much fat around the edge. Trim off excess fat, or it will drip and cause the coals to flare up. Cut through the edge of fat every 2.5cm/1in to prevent the meat from curling up. Choose steaks that are at least 2.5cm/1in thick so that the meat doesn't dry out and become tough.

To cook a steak: Season with salt and pepper. Brush grill with oil and place steak over the hottest part of the coals. Sear the steaks for 3 minutes on each side, searing the fat around the edges too. Then move steak to less intense heat or raise the grill and cook. For rare steaks allow another 4–5 minutes on each side; medium: 6–7 minutes on each side; and well-done 8–10 minutes on each side.

The meat will feel quite soft for rare steaks, but will become firmer as it gets well cooked, and the juices will run from red to clear when meat is pierced with the tip of a knife.

STEAK AU POIVRE
Serves 4

Deliciously peppery, but not fiery, these steaks are good with cream poured over them.

4 tablespoons black peppercorns
salt
4 rump steaks
oil
single cream (optional)

Crush the peppercorns roughly; hammer with a rolling pin through several sheets of greaseproof paper, or blend very quickly in a liquidiser or food processor. Do not crush to a powder. Place the peppercorns on a large plate and press the steaks down hard onto them. Lightly coat both sides. Sprinkle with salt. Brush with a little oil, then sear over very hot coals until brown. Turn the steaks with tongs so as not to dislodge too many peppercorns. Cook to taste and drizzle with a little single cream as you serve them, if liked.

MALAY BEEF
Serves 4

This needs a little preparation—preferably the day before—and then it cooks quickly over hot coals. Coconut and peppers give this a creamy, hot flavour. Don't worry if the marinade curdles.

300ml/½ pint milk
50g/2oz dessicated coconut
2.5-cm/1-in piece fresh root ginger
2 small chilli peppers
1 tablespoon dark brown sugar
½ teaspoon cayenne
4 small quick-fry tenderised beef steaks
salt and pepper

Place the milk and coconut in a small pan. Heat gently. Peel and very finely chop the ginger. Chop the chilli peppers. Add ginger, chilli, sugar and cayenne to the milk. Remove from the heat. Reserve 4 tablespoons of the marinade. Cut the steak into long 2.5-cm/1-in-wide strips. Season lightly with salt and pepper and lay meat in milk. Leave to marinate for 2 hours, overnight if possible. Thread the meat onto wooden or metal skewers or place carefully over a fine grill-rack. Grill over hot coals, basting with the marinade occasionally for 3–4 minutes on each side. Heat the remaining marinade and serve with the meat.

QUICK-FRIED STEAKS WITH BARBECUE GLAZE
Serves 6

Choose thick, tenderised quick-fry steaks, or they will dry out and char.

Barbecue Glaze
1 tablespoon malt vinegar
1 teaspoon mild English mustard
1 tablespoon dark brown sugar
pinch of paprika
2 teaspoons Worcestershire sauce
1 teaspoon soy sauce
3 tablespoons tomato ketchup

6 quick-fry tenderised steaks
salt and pepper
oil

Mix the barbecue glaze ingredients together with a little water to give a thin sauce. Sprinkle the steaks with salt and pepper and brush with oil. Sear over medium-hot coals for 1 minute on each side, brush with glaze and cook for a further 4–5 minutes on each side, brushing frequently with the glaze. Serve with a crisp salad and the remaining glaze.

JAPANESE BEEF
Serves 4

Buy the best possible braising steak or—better still—use sirloin.

1-cm/½-in piece fresh root ginger
1 garlic clove
2 tablespoons runny honey
2 tablespoons soy sauce
1 tablespoon dry sherry
sesame or corn oil
500g/1lb best braising steak
1 green pepper, sliced

Peel the ginger and grate finely. Crush the garlic. Place in a large shallow dish; add the honey, soy and sherry. Mix well. Cut the meat into thin strips. Add to the marinade and stir until meat is well coated. Cover and leave for 2 hours. Drain and thread the meat tightly onto skewers with the pepper. Grill over hot coals for 10–12 minutes, turning frequently. The meat should be brown and well-done at the edges, but the slices should remain pink at the centre. Serve with egg noodles.

RUSSIAN SHASHLIK
Serves 6-8

Red wine vinegar tenderises the beef, and coriander imparts a unique flavour.

1kg/2lb sirloin beef
1 onion
4 tablespoons red wine vinegar
1 teaspoon salt
½ teaspoon ground coriander
black pepper
100g/4oz button mushrooms
oil
1 lemon

Trim the meat of excess fat and cut into 2.5-cm/1-in cubes. Place in a a bowl. Peel and finely grate the onion; add to the bowl with the vinegar, salt, coriander, a good shake of pepper and the mushrooms. Turn the meat in the marinade; cover and leave overnight. Thread the meat and mushrooms together on metal skewers and brush with oil. Grill over hot coals for 10–15 minutes, turning and brushing frequently with oil. serve with wedges of lemon.

BEEF STRIPS WITH HORSERADISH

Serves 6

Freeze the meat until firm, then it is easy to slice thinly. Or buy prepared beef "olive" slices. Since this marinade is quite hot, serve with noodles or warm bread.

1 rump steak—about 5cm/2in thick, weighing about 350g/12oz
8 spring onions
4 tablespoons soy sauce
4 tablespoons dry sherry or saké
1 tablespoon creamed horseradish
oil

Trim the steak of excess fat. Freeze meat for 3 hours or until firm but not solid. Using a very sharp knife cut thin slices horizontally through the meat. Cut the spring onions in 2.5-cm/1-in lengths. Thread the steak and onions onto wooden or metal skewers, weaving the meat around the spring onions. Mix the soy sauce, sherry and horseradish together and brush liberally over meat. Leave for 30 minutes. Grill over hot coals for 2–3 minutes on each side until the meat turns brown and is just cooked. Brush with the marinade during cooking and serve with whatever marinade remains.

RED WINE MARINATED BEEF

Beef skirt or flank is ideal for barbecueing, but it is best eaten rare or medium rare as it is lean and can be dry. This marinade helps to tenderise the meat.

Marinade
1 onion
1 carrot
½ teaspoon dried parsley
½ teaspoon dried thyme
1 bay leaf
6 peppercorns
2 tablespoons oil
150ml/¼ pint red wine

4 thick slices beef skirt or flank steak
salt and pepper
oil

Peel and slice the onion and carrot. Place in a large shallow dish with the herbs, spices, oil and wine. Add the beef and turn it in the marinade until well coated. Leave for 6 hours, overnight if possible. Drain the meat, season with salt and pepper and sear over hot coals for 2–3 minutes on each side. Brush with oil; move to less intense heat (or move the grill-rack higher up) and cook for 5–6 minutes on each side. Serve with onion rings.

BURGERS

BASIC HAMBURGER
Serves 6

This is the basic beefburger recipe to which you can add all sorts of spices and seasonings.

1 onion
675g/1½lb lean minced beef
3 teaspoons salt
½ teaspoon pepper

Peel and finely chop the onion. Mix into the minced beef with the seasoning. Divide mixture into six. Pat each piece firmly into a neat round shape about 1cm/½in thick. chill for 1 hour. Grill over hot coals. For rare burgers allow 2 minutes each side; medium—4 minutes; and well-done—6 minutes each side. Serve with toasted bread rolls and relishes.

ECONOMICAL BURGER
Serves 6

This recipe helps stretch the beef a bit further—saving on money but not on flavour.

575g/1¼lb minced beef
50g/2oz breadcrumbs
1 onion, finely chopped
1 teaspoon Worcestershire sauce
1 tablespoon tomato purée
1 tablespoon fresh chopped parsley
1 teaspoon salt
½ teaspoon pepper

Make as for Basic hamburger.

VARIATIONS

Cheeseburgers: Add 50g/2oz grated mature Cheddar and 1 teaspoon English mustard to the basic mixture. Cook as before. Top with a slice of cheese and cook for a further 1–2 minutes, if desired.

Paprika burgers: Add 1 deseeded and finely chopped green pepper, 2 finely chopped spring onions, ½ teaspoon paprika and 1 tablespoon tomato purée to basic recipe. Top with sliced green pepper.

Hamburger au Poivre: Make Basic hamburgers omitting pepper and adding 2 teaspoons Worcestershire sauce and 1 teaspoon French mustard to the basic recipe. Shape burgers and chill. Coat each burger with coarsely ground black pepper. Serve with sliced tomato.

Herb and Capers: Add 2 tablespoons drained capers, 1 teaspoon sage, 1 teaspoon oregano, ½ teaspoon ground chilli pepper and 1 egg to the basic burger mixture. Shape and chill.

Spinachburgers: (Serves 6-8) Reduce salt to ½ teaspoon, omit tomato purée, and add 1-2 eggs. Press 10oz/275g frozen spinach into a sieve to remove water, and mix well with Economical burger mix. Shape and chill. Cook 5–6 minutes a side, if necessary on foil since these burgers are extra moist. Melt cheese on top for last minute cooking, if desired.

Curryburgers: Add 1 teaspoon mild curry powder, 1 chopped onion, 1 tablespoon chopped fresh mint, and 1 tablespoon lemon juice to Basic burger recipe. Top with coleslaw if liked.

LAMB BURGERS WITH ROSEMARY
Makes 8

Sweet, juicy lamb makes wonderful burgers, especially flavoured with garlic and rosemary. Don't add the garlic if you are freezing burgers as the flavour gets stronger.

1 clove garlic
2 onions
750g/1½lb miced lamb
1 tablespoon chopped fresh parsley (or 1 teaspoon dried)
1½ teaspoons chopped fresh rosemary (or ½ teaspoon dried)
½ teaspoon salt
good shake black pepper

Crush the garlic, peel and very finely chop the onion. Add to the lamb with the herbs and seasoning. Shape into eight burgers, about 2.5cm/1in thick. Chill. Grill over hot coals for about 5 minutes on each side.

CHICKPEA BURGERS

The people of Egypt make tiny chickpea balls (called Falafel) and then fry them. This method is more practical for barbecueing.

1 onion
two 396-g/14-oz cans cooked chickpeas
1 teaspoon salt
½ teaspoon pepper
2 tablespoons fresh coriander or parsley
¼ teaspoon cayenne
½ teaspoon ground coriander
50g/2oz fresh breadcrumbs
flour
oil

Peel and very finely chop the onion. Drain the chickpeas thoroughly, then place in a bowl and mash well with a potato masher or fork. Add the onion, seasonings and breadcrumbs and knead well together. Form into 5-cm/2-in rounds about 1cm/½in thick. Coat in flour. Chill until firm. Brush with oil, place on foil, and grill over hot coals for 4–5 minutes on each side. Serve with tomato sauce.

SAUSAGES

BARBECUED SAUSAGE AND BACON SKEWERS

Makes 8 skewers

A popular barbecue combination for adults and kids alike.

250g/8oz streaky bacon rashers
500g/1lb pork sausages
8 firm tomatoes
1 quantity Basic barbecue sauce (page 56)

Remove rind and bone from bacon. Cut each rasher in half and roll up each piece. Cut each sausage into 3 pieces. Cut tomatoes into quarters. Skewer bacon, sausages and tomatoes together and brush with barbecue sauce. Grill over hot coals for 10 minutes turning and brushing with the sauce occasionally. Serve with any remaining barbecue sauce.

CUMBERLAND SAUSAGE GRILL

These wonderful traditional Cumberland sausages look spectacular and feed about six hungry people. Simply place two metal skewers through the sausage to prevent it uncurling and grill over hot coals for 15–20 minutes, turning frequently to prevent the skin from bursting or burning. Remove the skewers and slice the sausage to serve.

BLACK OR WHITE PUDDINGS

These are delicious cooked over a barbecue, but do tend to crumble, so cut the puddings into 2.5-cm/1-in thick slices and cook quickly over medium-hot coals for 2–3 minutes only on each side. Garnish with sprigs of fresh sage.

GERMAN BRATWURST

These long, thin sausages are lightly spiced and need about 15 minutes grilling over hot coals, turning until golden brown.

POLISH OR DUTCH BOILING RINGS

These horseshoe-shaped sausages are pre-cooked with a slightly smoky flavour and need just 10–15 minutes cooking over hot coals to heat them through. Serve sliced.

KABANOS AND PINEAPPLE KEBABS

Makes 8 kebabs

Kabanos are long, thin, highly-smoked, chewy pork sausages, flavoured with hot spice and garlic. They give a lovely tang to the chicken.

3 Kabanos
1 small can pineapple chunks
2 chicken breasts, cooked
1 tablespoon oil

Cut the kabanos into 2.5-cm/1-in pieces. Drain the pineapple. Cut the chicken into 2.5-cm/1-in chunks. Thread kabanos, pineapple and chicken together onto small metal skewers and brush with oil. Grill over hot coals for 10 minutes, turning and brushing with oil occasionally.

LENTIL SAUSAGES

Makes 8-10

Cooked over a barbecue, these pick up a smoky flavour. It is important to make sure the lentil and cracked wheat mixture is cooked until the water is absorbed, or the mixture will be too wet and soft to hold together.

175g/6oz brown lentils
1½ teaspoons salt
100g/4oz pre-cooked cracked wheat
   (pourgouri)
200ml/7fl oz oil
1 onion
2 spring onions
2 tablespoons fresh parsley
½ teaspoon black pepper
½ teaspoon paprika
1 egg

Wash and drain the lentils. Place in a large saucepan, cover with 900ml/1½ pints water; add the salt and bring to the boil. Simmer for 30 minutes or until tender. Stir in the cracked wheat and 5 tablespoons oil. Simmer for a further 3–4 minutes. Turn off the heat, cover and leave for 15 minutes or until all the water has been absorbed. Very finely chop the onion, spring onion, and parsley. Add to the lentil mixture, with the pepper, paprika and egg. Mash well or blend in a food processor until smooth. Using damp hands roll the mixture into sausage shapes about 3in long. Chill until firm. Grill over hot coals for about 3 minutes on each side.

OFFAL

If you haven't tried cooking liver, kidneys or even heart over charcoal, you'll be surprised at the result. Barbecueing seals the outside—allowing the inside of the meat to stay juicy, tender and rare. Lamb's liver, kidney or heart, calves' livers or kidneys, or pigs' kidneys are the ideal offal to grill. The pieces should be thin enough to cook quickly, but not so thin that it will overcook and dry out. Brush well with oil and herbs or spices to help flavour and moisten the meat.

LIVER WITH LEMON, SAGE AND BLACK PEPPER
Serves 6

Cook this liver carefully so that it remains moist and tender. The lemon and sage make a delicate complement to lamb's liver.

500g/1lb lamb's liver, thinly sliced
3 tablespoons lemon juice
salt
freshly ground black pepper
2 sprigs fresh sage (or ¼ teaspoon dried sage)
2 tablespoons oil
2 tablespoons butter, melted

Brush the liver liberally with lemon juice; sprinkle with a little salt and a lot of black pepper. Very finely chop the sage and add to the oil and butter. Brush over the liver. Grill over medium-hot coals for 6 minutes on each side, brushing well with oil and butter. Test with a skewer; the meat juices will run clear when the liver is cooked.

ROSEMARY-GRILLED KIDNEYS WITH ORANGE BUTTER
Serves 6

These are tasty and succulent—take care not to overcook them.

6 lamb's kidneys
6 small branches fresh rosemary
4 tablespoons olive oil
1 teaspoon dried mixed herbs
grated rind of 1 orange
50g/2oz butter, softened
salt and pepper

Remove fat and membrane from the kidneys. Cut through the rounded back of the kidney towards the core, but do not cut right in half. Open out the kidney to make it flat. Remove rosemary leaves from the branches, leaving just a few at the top. Chop the leaves and push the branches right through the kidney to hold it open. Place them in a shallow dish. Add the chopped rosemary to the oil with mixed herbs, and pour over the kidneys. Leave for 30 minutes to marinate. Beat the orange rind into the butter with a little black pepper. Chill. Drain the kidneys and season with a little salt and pepper. Grill over medium-hot coals for 3–5 minutes on each side, brushing with the oil marinade to prevent them drying out. Serve topped with a little orange butter.

FISH

SIMPLE GRILLED FISH
Serves 4

Choose small whole fresh fish such as mackerel, herring, trout, sardines. red mullet. Rinse and gut each one. Sprinkle the cavity with salt and black pepper and place a bay leaf inside. Place the fish in an oiled hinged basket and grill over hot coals for about 4–5 minutes on each side, or until the skin browns and blisters. Squeeze lemon juice over each fish and serve.

GARLIC-BUTTERED PRAWNS
Serves 4

Leave the shells on the prawns to protect them from too much heat. Buy raw prawns if you can and cook them a minute or two longer.

Marinade
2 tablespoons olive oil
25g/1oz butter, melted
1 clove garlic, crushed
1 tablespoon lemon juice
1 tablespoon chopped fresh parsley
350g/12oz large whole cooked prawns

Mix the marinade ingredients together; place in a shallow dish and add the prawns. Stir until well coated. Leave for 2 hours then thread prawns onto small metal or wooden skewers and grill over medium-hot coals for 3 minutes on each side or until the prawn shells turn golden.

SALMON WITH DILL
Serves 4

Deliciously simple. Cook the salmon steaks on foil if they are thin, or they may fall apart.

4 salmon steaks
4 tablespoons sunflower oil
6 sprigs fresh dill (or 1 teaspoon dried)
salt and pepper
1 lemon
½ cucumber, sliced

Lay the salmon steaks in a shallow dish, pour over the oil. Top with dill and sprinkle with salt and pepper. Cut the lemon in half. Squeeze the juice from one half over the salmon. Cut the other half into 4 thick slices, reserve for garnish. Marinate the salmon for 30 minutes, then grill over medium hot coals for about 6 minutes on each side, turning and brushing with the marinade occasionally. Take care not to overcook the salmon, or it will begin to break up. When the flesh has turned pink and is firm, it will be cooked. Serve on a bed of sliced cucumber with the lemon slices.

SPICED MACKEREL
Serves 4

Buy firm, fresh fish and prepare this in advance.

4 small mackerel or 2 large
1 tablespoon tomato purée
4 tablespoons oil
4 tablespoons lemon juice
1 teaspoon salt
shake of black pepper
½ teaspoon chilli pepper
pinch of cinnamon
pinch of ground coriander
pinch of ground cumin

Rinse and gut the fish. Cut off heads if not desired. Mix remaining ingredients together in a shallow dish. Add the fish and rub both inside and outside of fish with marinade. Cover and leave for at least 2 hours. Grill over hot coals for 5–7 minutes on each side turning the mackerel carefully. (Place the fish in a hinged wire basket if possible.) Do not overcook, or the fish will dry and fall apart. Serve with wedges of lemon, salad and fresh brown bread.

ALMOND-STUFFED TROUT
Serves 4

Prepare the stuffing in advance, but do not add it until just before cooking.

4 medium-sized trout
grated rind and juice of 1 lemon
100g/4oz flaked almonds
salt and black pepper
pinch ground cumin
1 tablespoon chopped fresh parsley (or 1 teaspoon dried)
4 bay leaves
oil

Rinse and gut the fish. Mix the lemon rind and juice, almonds, a good shake of salt and pepper, cumin and parsley together. Pack into the fish and place a bay leaf on top of each one. Tie up the fish with a little string to prevent it from opening, or place in a hinged wire basket. Brush fish with oil. Grill over medium-hot coals for 10 minutes on each side or until the skin begins to split and the flesh looks pale and firm. Brush with oil occasionally; scatter with almonds.

BARBECUED TROUT WITH LEMON
Serves 4

Now that trout is so widely farmed it is cheap and easy to buy. This is the most succulent way to cook them. Check occasionally during cooking so as not to overcook them.

4 large fresh rainbow trout
salt and black pepper
4 bay leaves
4 slices lemon
4 sprigs parsley
50g/2oz butter

Rinse and gut the fish. Sprinkle the cavity with salt and pepper, place a bay leaf, a slice of lemon and a sprig of parsley inside each fish. Wrap the fish tightly in buttered foil. Place over medium-hot coals and cook for 30–40 minutes until the flesh feels firm and will fall away from the bone.

ORIENTAL FISH
Serves 4

This Japanese-style marinade is delicious brushed over any white fish fillets, small whole fish or kebabs.

6 tablespoons soy sauce
1 clove garlic, crushed
2 tablespoons sesame oil
2 tablespoons brown sugar
2 tablespoons lemon juice
pinch of ginger
3 small plaice, sole, or dabs
1 spring onion, chopped

Mix soy, garlic, oil, sugar, lemon and ginger together and pour into a shallow dish. Lay the fish on top, turn it in the marinade to coat and leave for 1 hour. Cover the grill with greased foil and place fish on top. Grill over hot coals for 4–5 minutes on each side. Sprinkle with spring onion and serve.

BACON-SCALLOP SKEWERS
Serves 8

Scallops and bacon are always favourites. Prepare them in advance; cover, and then they take just 5 minutes to cook.

8 scallops
8 rashers streaky bacon
juice of 1 lemon
50g/2oz butter, melted
1 tablespoon chopped fresh parsley

Cut the scallops and bacon rashers in half. Roll up each piece of bacon. Thread scallops and bacon rolls alternately onto metal skewers. Sprinkle each with lemon juice and brush with butter. Grill over hot coals for 5 minutes, turning and basting frequently with butter. Sprinkle with parsley. Serve with brown bread and butter.

PIRI PIRI FISH KEBABS
Makes 6

This marinade is quite spicy and hot—delicious on prawns too. Buy chilli sauce from delicatessens or continental stores; it is perfect for barbecued food.

675g/1½lb firm white fish, i.e. monk fish
1 onion
1 small red pepper
1 small yellow pepper
1 teaspoon hot chilli sauce
3 tablespoons corn oil
1 clove garlic, crushed
2 teaspoons brown sugar
bay leaves

Skin and bone the fish. Cut into 2.5-cm/1-in pieces. Peel onion, cut into wedges, and separate leaves. Cut peppers in half, discard core and seeds and cut peppers into 2.5-cm/1-in squares. Thread fish, onion and peppers alternately onto metal skewers. Mix chilli sauce, corn oil, garlic and sugar together. Brush over the fish and grill over medium-hot coals for 10 minutes, turning and brushing with the marinade ocassionally. Serve together with cucumber and wedges of lemon.

FISH PARCELS
Serves 4

Buy either fresh fillets or frozen steaks for this recipe, which is almost a complete meal.

4 cod or haddock steaks
salt and pepper
4 button mushrooms
½ small onion
4 tomatoes
25g/1oz peas
25g/1oz butter
1 tablespoon lemon juice

Place each fish steak on a square of foil. Sprinkle with salt and pepper. Slice the mushrooms; peel and very finely chop the onion; chop the tomatoes. Divide the mushrooms, onion, tomato and peas over the fish steaks. Dot with butter and sprinkle with lemon juice. Wrap the foil loosely around the fish, making sure the folds are tightly sealed. Place over hot coals and cook for 20–30 minutes. Serve sprinkled with chopped parsley.

SMOKED FISHCAKES
Makes 10

Use boil-in-the-bag haddock for speed, or poach the fish in milk, using milk later to make a white sauce.

350-g/12-oz packet frozen boil-in-the-bag smoked haddock
350g/12oz cold cooked mashed potato
2 tablespoons chopped fresh coriander or parsley
pinch of paprika
salt and black pepper
oil

Cook the haddock as directed on the packet. Drain and flake the flesh; add to the mashed potato with the coriander or parsley, paprika, and salt and black pepper. Mash well together with a fork, adding enough egg to bind the mixture to a firm paste. Using floured hands shape the mixture into ten flat, neat fish cakes about 8cm/2½in round. Place on a floured tray and chill for 30 minutes. Cover the grill-rack with foil. Brush the fish cakes with a little oil and grill over medium-hot coals for 5–8 minutes on each side, carefully using a fish slice to turn them over. Serve with shies of lemon, and parsley.

VEGETABLES

BAKED POTATOES

No barbecue or bonfire is complete without baked potatoes. I like them buried as they are in the hot coals until the skins blacken and burn and the inside is soft and fluffy—they really do pick up a barbecued flavour—but unfortunately the skins are almost inedible! If you want to eat your fibre, wrap medium-sized, scrubbed potatoes in foil. Bury the potatoes in hot coals and cook for about 40–50 minutes—depending on size. Pierce with a skewer and remove the potatoes when they feel soft.

Note: The potatoes will cook more quickly if first parboiled in their skins in salted water for 10 minutes.

BAKED POTATO TOPPINGS

For 4 potatoes

Have bowls of toppings ready and waiting to be spooned over piping-hot jacket potatoes.

Blue Cheese and Walnut: Mash 50g/2oz Danish Blue cheese; stir in 2 tablespoons single cream and 3 tablespoons milk to give a soft, creamy consistency. Add 25g/1oz chopped walnuts.

Sour Cream and Chives: Stir 1 tablespoon freshly chopped (or dried) chives into 150ml/¼ pint sour cream. Season with salt and pepper.

Bacon and Pineapple: Finely chop 1 onion. Snip 4 rashers streaky bacon into small pieces, fry together in a little oil until crispy. Chop 2 small rings of canned pineapple and add to bacon and onion.

Curry Mayonnaise: Mix together 1 teaspoon mild curry paste, 2 tablespoons mango chutney, and 4 tablespoons of mayonnaise.

POTATO SKINS

Bake potatoes in their jackets. Scoop out the potato and keep the skins. (Use the scooped out potato later for mash.) Brush inside the skins with melted butter and place them cut side downwards on the grill over medium coals. Cook for 10–15 minutes until crisp. Take care not to let them burn.

MARMITE POTATO SLICES

Serves 6

These are like huge savoury crisps and quite quick to cook.

3 large potatoes
50g/2oz butter
2 tablespoons oil
2 teaspoons Marmite

Scrub the potatoes but do not peel. Parboil in salted water for 8–10 minutes. Drain and slice thickly. Heat the butter, oil and Marmite together in a frying pan. Brush over the potatoes and grill above hot coals for about 5 minutes on each side or until crisp and golden.

CHEESE AND POTATO HASH
Serves 4

Choose a mature cheese to give this a good flavour.

1kg/2lb potatoes
225g/8oz Double Gloucester cheese
1 onion
salt and pepper

Peel the potatoes and cut into 1-cm/½-in cubes. Parboil in salted water for 3 minutes. Drain well. Chop cheese into 1-cm/½-in cubes. Peel and finely chop onion. Cut four 30-cm/12-in squares of foil. Divide potato, cheese and onion between foil; season and make foil parcels, securing edges tightly. Place over hot coals and cook for 20 minutes until potato is tender when pierced with a skewer.

POTATOES LYONNAISE
Serves 6–8

A classic recipe that can even be cooked on a barbecue.

1kg/2lb potatoes
25g/1oz butter
3 tablespoons cooking oil
2 large onions
½ teaspoon salt
pepper
1 tablespoon chopped fresh parsley

Peel potatoes and cook in boiling salted water for 10 minutes. Drain and allow to cool. Cut into thin slices. Peel and thinly slice onions. Melt butter and oil together in a large frying pan; add the onions and fry for 2–3 minutes until onions become transparent. Add potatoes, seasoning and parsley; stir well. Divide mixture in half and place each onto large squares of double-thickness foil. Bring the edges up together and seal tightly, leaving room for the expansion of steam. Place over hot coals for 45–50 minutes or until potatoes feel tender when pierced with a skewer.

FRESH CORN ON THE COB

Designed for barbecueing—corn on the cob has its own protective cover to prevent it from burning.

For each corn cob: Turn back the husks from the corn and remove the silky hairs. Brush the corn with melted butter (or use Garlic butter, see page 56) and season with a little salt and pepper. Replace the husks and secure ends with a little string or cotton thread. Cook on the barbecue rack over hot coals for 40 minutes–1 hour, turning occasionally, or until tender. Remove the husks using oven gloves and serve with melted butter.

Frozen corn on the cob: Place each cob on a sheet of heavy-duty foil and brush with melted butter. Wrap securely and cook in the hot barbecue coals for 15–20 minutes.

GARLIC -STUFFED MUSHROOMS
Makes 6

These are tasty as a vegetable and great as a starter, too. They can be prepared hours in advance and are then quick to cook.

2 tablespoons olive oil
2 tablespoons lemon juice
6 large round mushroom caps
salt and pepper
1 large onion
2 cloves garlic
50g/2oz butter
4 tablespoons parsley
50g/2oz breadcrumbs

Mix the oil, lemon juice and a little salt and pepper together in a large bowl. Add the mushrooms, toss together and leave for 2–3 hours. Peel and very finely chop the onion. Peel and crush the garlic. Melt the butter in a small pan, and gently fry the onion and garlic for 5 minutes or until the onion is transparent. Remove from the heat. Stir in the breadcrumbs and chopped parsley. Drain the mushroom marinade into the breadcrumbs. Mix well then pack the stuffing into the mushroom caps. Place on a tray, cover and leave until ready to cook. Cook over medium-hot coals for 8–10 minutes or until heated through.

MUSHROOMS WITH BLUE CHEESE

Delicious as a starter or as an accompaniment to a main meal.

225g/8oz mushrooms
oil
100g/4oz Cambazola or blue Brie
fresh mint or basil

Brush the mushrooms well with oil. Cut the cheese into small pieces and place a little into each mushroom. Grill over hot coals for 5–10 minutes. Garnish with a fresh leaf of mint or basil.

TOMATOES

These are always popular with grilled or barbecued food. The simplest way to cook them is to cut them in half and grill them cut side down for a few minutes, then turn them over and continue cooking until tender. They are delicious brushed with a little Spiced oil (page 56), melted butter, or garlic butter. Spike with fresh rosemary or sprinkle generously with chopped parsley or basil, and ground black pepper. Sweet cherry tomatoes can simply be skewered and quickly grilled until hot.

TOMATO AND ONION GRILL
Serves 6

Use large beef tomatoes which are "meatier" and sweeter than the smaller ones and will not fall apart. Use the Spanish onions which are sweeter, too.

2 beef tomatoes
2 large onions
2 tablespoons olive oil
a few sprigs fresh thyme

Slice the tomatoes and onions thickly. Lay them on the base of a hinged wire basket or place on a sheet of foil over the grill-rack. Brush with oil; top with sprigs of thyme and season with salt and pepper. Close the basket and grill over hot coals. Cook for about 3 minutes on each side.

STUFFED TOMATOES
Serves 4

Use the same stuffing mixture for Garlic-stuffed mushrooms, or follow this more unusual Italian recipe. These tomatoes make a delicious starter.

4 firm tomatoes
1 clove garlic
25g/1oz breadcrumbs
50g/2oz Italian Blue Cheese: Gorgonzola or Dolcelatte
2 sprigs fresh rosemary or pinch of dried rosemary
1 tablespoon oil

Cut tops off of tomatoes. Scoop out and discard core and seeds. Finely chop garlic and mix with the breadcrumbs. Crumble the blue cheese into the breadcrumbs. Snip the rosemary leaves into small pieces and add to stuffing with the oil. Stir well together and pack into the tomatoes. Replace lids. Wrap each tomato tightly in foil and cook over hot coals for 10–15 minutes until tender.

AUBERGINE AND ANCHOVY FANS
Serves 4

Impressive and savoury, these can be prepared in advance. Choose small aubergines for this recipe or they will take too long to cook. Half an aubergine is plenty per person!

2 aubergines
4 tomatoes
2 small onions
4 tablespoons Spiced oil (page 56) or cooking oil
2 bay leaves
4 anchovy fillets

Leaving the aubergine whole, and using a sharp knife, cut the vegetable into slices, taking care not to cut right through the stalk. Brush between each slice with oil and place each on a double square of foil. Slice the tomatoes. Peel the onions and cut into wafer-thin slices. Finely chop the anchovy fillets. Divide tomato, onion and anchovy between each slice. Season with salt and pepper and place a bay leaf on each aubergine. Wrap foil around and fold edges tightly. Cook directly on hot coals for 20 minutes or until tender.

ITALIAN-STYLE COURGETTES
Serves 4

Almost a vegetable pizza, these will be a popular vegetable with a barbecue meal. Parboil the courgettes in advance.

4 courgettes
4 tablespoons tomato relish
4 tablespoons Parmesan cheese
freshly ground black pepper

Parboil the courgettes in salted water for just 4 minutes. Drain and cut in half lengthways. Place cut side down on the barbecue grill and cook for 4–5 minutes. Turn over and spread each with tomato relish. Sprinkle with Parmesan and pepper, cook for a further 5–10 minutes until tender.

MARINATED VEGETABLE KEBABS
Makes 6

Mediterranean in flavour, this is a tasty and simple way to cook vegetables with your other barbecued foods.

Marinade
1 small onion
2 cloves garlic
6 tablespoons corn oil
1 teaspoon dried mixed herbs
grated rind of 1 orange
good shake of salt and pepper
2 courgettes
1 small red pepper
1 small green pepper
1 small aubergine
100g/4oz button mushrooms
1 can artichoke hearts, drained

Peel and grate the onion and crush the garlic. Add to the oil with the herbs, orange rind, salt and pepper, and place in a large shallow dish. Cut the courgettes into 2.5-cm/1-in lengths. Cut peppers in half, discard core and seeds and cut into 2.5-cm/1-in squares. Cut aubergine into 2.5-cm/1-in cubes. Wipe mushrooms. Cut artichokes into quarters. Place vegetables in the marinade; stir until well coated. Thread onto metal skewers and grill over hot coals for 10–15 minutes, turning and basting with the marinade until the vegetables are browned.

RATATOUILLE
Serves 6–8

Delicious served hot or cold, this is the perfect vegetable accompaniment to nearly all barbecued meats. Cook it on the barbecue, or make it in advance and just reheat. The quantity of ingredients can be varied according to what's available at the time.

25g/1oz butter
3 tablespoons cooking oil
1 clove garlic, crushed
2 small aubergines, sliced
1 green pepper, sliced and deseeded
1 red pepper, sliced and deseeded
5 courgettes, sliced
one 395-g/14-oz can peeled tomatoes
1 teaspoon dried basil
2 bay leaves
½ teaspoon salt
pepper

Melt the butter and oil together in a large frying pan. Add the garlic and aubergine and fry for 3–4 minutes until aubergine has softened. Add the peppers, courgettes, tomatoes, herbs and seasoning. Stir well together and bring to the boil. Place the frying pan over hot coals and cook, stirring occasionally for 20–30 minutes. Alternatively, place the mixture on a double thickness of foil; bring the edges up together and seal very tightly. Place it among hot coals to cook for 15–20 minutes. Serve in a casserole dish.

HOT BREAD & CHEESE

PITTA BREAD

Hot pitta bread makes an ideal pocket to stuff with salad and sliced barbecue meat or kebabs. To heat them up, sprinkle each pitta bread with a little water and place over medium-hot coals until the bread puffs up. Take care not to burn the bread. Using a sharp knife, cut along one side of the bread and open up the pocket. This bread is delicious cut into strips and dunked into dips, too.

GARLIC BREAD

Serves 4

The favourite hot bread to have with barbecued food. If you are making a lot for a party, also make some without the garlic for those who are not so keen!

1 French bread stick
1–2 cloves garlic
75g/3oz butter, softened
black pepper
1 teaspoon dried rosemary
2 tablespoons chopped fresh parsley,
    OR 2 tablespoons dried

Using a sharp knife cut the bread into thick slices, taking care not to cut right through the bread. Peel and finely crush the garlic; beat into the butter with the pepper and herbs. Spread between the bread slices, and wrap tightly in a large sheet of buttered foil. Place over hot coals and cook for 10 minutes on each side.

SAVOURY GRILLED CHEESE

Serves 8

Seasoned melting cheese is delicious. Make sure you use only firm cheese, and don't overcook or it will melt away.

225g/8oz firm cheese such as Gruyère, Emmental, Edam or Gouda
1 tablespoon olive oil
2 teaspoons wine vinegar
pinch of mustard powder
salt and black pepper
½ teaspoon dried mixed herbs

Cut the cheese into cubes about 2.5cm/1in thick. Beat the oil, vinegar, mustard powder, salt and pepper and herbs together. Brush a little over each cube of cheese. Grill over medium-hot coals for about 1 minute. Carefully turn over the cheese slices using a metal fish slice. Cook for a further minute until the cheese just softens and begins to bubble. Place on warm plates and serve with warm, crusty bread.

MOZZARELLA AND SALAMI STUFFED BREAD

Serves 4–8

Almost like a pizza, this is irresistible and makes a good starter.

1 large French bread stick
100g/4oz mozzarella cheese
stoned black olives
50g/2oz sliced salami

Using a sharp knife, cut the bread into thick slices without cutting right through the bread. Cut the mozzarella and olives into thin slices. Insert a slice each of mozzarella and salami and an olive between each bread slice. Wrap the loaf in a large sheet of buttered foil and seal tightly. Place over hot coals and heat for 10 minutes on each side. Unwrap and cut between slices.

BARBECUED SANDWICHES

You need a moist but firm filling in barbecued sandwiches, or they will fall apart.

Butter the bread on both sides and fill with paté, slices of blue cheese, cheese spread, shrimp or salmon paste, or mashed corned beef. For sweet fillings, use jam, chocolate spread or peanut butter. Grill on foil over medium-hot coals and cook for 1–2 minutes on each side until golden. Cut in half and serve.

PAPADUMS

These crisp, thin Indian pancakes are wonderful with spicy Indian-style barbecue foods and great to nibble at too. Brush plain or spiced papadums with oil and place over hot coals until they rise and crispen. Turn over and cook the other side. This will take only seconds. Take care not to allow them to brown or burn.

SWEET SWEETS

CHOCOLATE GONE BANANAS

Fun for all the family—simply make a small slit in the banana skin and insert one or two squares of chocolate. Wrap each banana in foil and cook directly on the coals for about 10 minutes. Don't be put off by the blackened skins; the fruit is delicious when split open. If liked, just barbecue unpeeled bananas without the chocolate or foil in the same way. Split the bananas open and eat with a teaspoon. Maple syrup makes a nice accompaniment too.

BARBADOS BAKED PINEAPPLE

Freshly grated coconut makes this dessert something special, but desiccated coconut is also good. Simply cut a fresh pineapple into rings. Place each onto a square of foil, and sprinkle with a little brown sugar and pinch of ginger. Top with grated coconut. Wrap the foil around and seal. Grill over warm coals for 10–15 minutes. Serve on individual plates, garnished with strawberries.

TOFFEE TEA CAKES

Cut 4 teacakes into 2.5-cm/1-in cubes and thread onto metal skewers. Mix together 50g/2oz melted butter, 3 tablespoons golden syrup and 1 tablespoon lemon juice; brush over the bread and grill over hot coals for 5–10 minutes until crisp and golden.

MULLED PEARS

Serves 4

These pears are somehow warming and comforting at the end of a chilly evening; prepare the pears in the morning and dip in lemon juice to prevent browning.

4 small ripe pears
4 teaspoons demerara sugar
12 cloves
4 tablespoons redcurrant jelly
grated rind of 1 orange

Peel halve and core the pears. Place each pear on 2 large squares of foil. Mix together demerara sugar, redcurrant jelly and orange rind. Spoon between 2 pear halves. Spike each with 4 cloves and wrap the foil around the pear, securing tightly at the top. Place the pears amongst the hot coals and cook for 30 minutes until tender. Serve hot with cream.

GOLDEN BAKED APPLES

An old favourite that cooks perfectly on a barbecue. Serve with lashings of whipped cream or ice cream.

4 medium cooking apples
50g/2oz butter

Nut and Raisin Filling
50g/2oz brown sugar
2 teaspoons cinnamon
25g/1oz walnuts, chopped
25g/1oz raisins
OR
Apricot and Ginger Filling
50g/2oz apricots, finely chopped
25g/1oz stem or crystallised ginger, chopped
50g/2oz brown sugar

Core the apples. Place each on a square of foil. Combine filling ingredients and fill the apples with the mixture. Dot apples with butter and wrap in foil, covering and sealing tightly. Then wrap each in another piece of foil. Barbecue directly on hot coals turning once or twice for 20–30 minutes or until tender.

SATSUMAS WITH RUM AND RAISIN
Serves 6

Buy large satsumas, clementines or tangerines with loose peel, and add a complementary liqueur.

6 large satsumas
50g/2oz raisins
2 tablespoons brown sugar
3 tablespoons rum

Using a sharp knife, carefully cut around the circumference of the satsumas, just cutting the peel and not the fruit. Ease away the top half of the peel and discard. Remove white pith from the fruit, but leave the fruit intact in its orange peel cup. Mix together the raisins and sugar and push into the centre of each satsuma. Pour a little rum over each. Place the satsumas on large squares of foil; bring the foil up over each and twist to secure. Place satsumas amongst warm coals and cook for 15 minutes. Unwrap and serve with cream.

ALMOND-STUFFED APRICOTS
Serves 6

Simple to prepare, simple to cook, and simply delicious.

5 tablespoons ground almonds
3 tablespoons castor sugar
1 tablespoon almond liqueur
25g/1oz glacé cherries
396-g/14-oz can apricot halves in natural juices
2 tablespoons redcurrant jelly

Mix the ground almonds, sugar and liqueur together to give a soft paste. Drain the apricots well and reserve the juice. Place a little almond mixture in the centre of each apricot, topped with a cherry. Place on foil and heat over warm coals for 15 minutes or until hot. Place the juice and redcurrant jelly in a small pan; stand it amongst the coals and heat the juice. Serve apricots with a little juice and some single cream.

DARK CHOCOLATE SAUCE

Delicious served warm, this sauce will thicken when chilled. Store in the refrigerator for up to 1 week.

50g/2oz butter
25g/1oz cocoa
3 tablespoons golden syrup

Melt the ingredients together in a saucepan over a low heat. Stir until smooth.

MARASCHINO AND MALLOW KEBABS

One for the kids and softies at heart! Thread pink and white marshmallows alternately onto metal skewers with maraschino cherries. Hold them over warm coals for 1 or 2 minutes until the marshmallows just turn golden. (Do not allow them to touch the bars of the grill or you'll end up with a sticky mess.) Remove from skewers before serving. Serve dipped into Dark Chocolate Sauce (see recipe below).

FRUIT KEBABS WITH HONEY-LEMON SAUCE

Make up these easy fruit kebabs using any combination of fresh or canned fruits. Or why not prepare bowls of fruit and leave guests to thread up their own choice?

Choose from:
peach slices
apricot halves
wedges of apple and chunks of peeled bananas
  (dip in lemon juice to prevent browning)
pineapple chunks
green or black seedless grapes
strawberries or stoned dates

Sauce
6 tablespoons clear honey
2 tablespoon lemon juice

Make sure the pieces of fruit are of uniform size. Thread onto skewers. Gently heat honey and lemon juice together in a small pan and brush over fruit before cooking. Grill over warm coals until hot, about 5 minutes. Serve with remaining sauce.

MARINADES, SAUCES & EXTRAS

BASIC RED WINE MARINADE

This simple marinade can be used for any beef or lamb cut; it adds flavour and helps keep the meat moist during hot, dry grilling. Let the meat marinate for at least 3 hours for maximum effect.

150ml/¼ pint red wine
150ml/¼ pint light cooking oil: sunflower, soya or olive oil
2 cloves garlic, crushed
1 teaspoon sea salt
1 sprig fresh marjoram or pinch dried
1 sprig fresh rosemary or pinch dried
1 sprig fresh thyme or pinch dried
4 tablespoons chopped fresh parsley
1 teaspoon black pepper
2 bay leaves
1 small onion, sliced

Mix all the ingredients well together. The marinade is best used on the day it is made.

OIL MARINADE

Make sure you use good quality oil such as olive oil, sunflower, safflower or soya oil to flavour the food. Ideal for pork, chicken and vegetables.

150ml/¼ pint oil
1 clove garlic (optional)
1 small onion
1 bay leaf
2 teaspoons chopped fresh parsley
grated rind of 1 lemon
2 teaspoons lemon juice
salt and black pepper

Place the oil in a large shallow dish. Peel and slice the garlic and onion; place in the dish with the bay leaf, parsley, lemon rind and juice. Sprinkle with salt and pepper. Lay the food in the marinade; cover and leave for 2 hours.

BOSTON BAKED BEANS
Serves 10–12

A satisfying accompaniment to barbecued food.

25g/1oz butter
1 onion, finely chopped
one 580-g/1.28-lb can baked beans
2 tablespoons black treacle
1 tablespoon English mustard
pepper

Melt butter in a saucepan; add onion and fry until transparent. Add beans, treacle, mustard and a good shake of black pepper. Stir well and simmer gently.

SWEETCORN AND CUCUMBER RELISH

Sweet and crunchy, this relish should be made at least 2 hours before serving.

2 sticks celery
½ cucumber
200-g/7-oz can sweetcorn niblets
4 tablespoons cider vinegar
2 tablespoons vegetable oil
1 tablespoon sugar
½ teaspoon salt
½ teaspoon celery, cumin, OR coriander seeds

Dice the celery and cucumber finely; drain the sweetcorn and mix with the remaining ingredients. Place in a serving bowl and refrigerate for 2 hours before serving. Serve with hot or cold meats and with salads. Store in the fridge for up to 3 days.

PEPPER RELISH

This relish is cooked; if you want to keep it for long periods of time, bottle it while hot in sterilised screw-top jars and keep in the refrigerator for up to 3 months.

4 firm tomatoes
1 onion
1 green pepper
2 fresh green chillies
2 stalks celery
1 teaspoon salt
½ teaspoon ginger
½ teaspoon cinnamon
pinch of ground cloves
4 tablespoons pickling vinegar
4 tablespoons brown sugar

Peel, deseed and chop tomatoes. Peel and chop onion. Dice pepper and chillies discarding core seeds and white pith. (Take care not to touch the face or eyes after chopping the chillies.) Finely chop celery. Place all ingredients in a medium saucepan and bring to the boil. Lower the heat and simmer gently for 1 hour. Serve hot or cold. Store in an airtight container in the refrigerator for up to 2 weeks. Serve with barbecued and cold meats.

PIQUANT TOMATO RELISH
8–10 portions

This crisp, fresh relish sharpens burgers, sausages, and most barbecued meats.

1kg/2lb tomatoes
½ cucumber
4 sticks celery
6–8 small gherkins

Dressing
4 tablespoons vegetable oil
2 tablespoons malt vinegar
1 teaspoon salt
½ teaspoon dry mustard
½ teaspoon caster sugar
a few shakes of Tabasco sauce (optional)

Place tomatoes in a bowl and cover with boiling water. Leave for 1 minute; drain, then peel. Roughly chop the tomatoes; place in a medium-sized bowl. Dice the cucumber into 5-mm/¼-in cubes. Wash and slice celery; slice gherkins. Add to chopped tomatoes. Mix dressing ingredients together; add to tomato mixture and stir until well coated. Cover and leave in a cool place for 1 hour. The relish can be kept in a plastic container in a refrigerator for up to 1 week.

FLAVOURED BUTTERS

Make plenty of mustard, herb or lemon butters to serve over simple barbecued steaks or chops—just to add a touch more flavour.

to 225g/8oz softened butter add:

Lemon or Orange butter: Beat the finely grated rind and juice of 2 lemons or 2 oranges into the butter.

Black Pepper: Add 3 tablespoons coarsley-ground black peppercorns.

Garlic and Herbs: Crush 2 cloves of garlic to a pulp with 2 teaspoons salt. Beat into the butter with 4 tablespoons finely chopped fresh parsley, chives, rosemary or thyme.

BASIC BARBECUE SAUCE

A quick, easy sauce that is delicious spread over pork spareribs before cooking; it's good cold, too, just spooned over hot sausages or burgers.

4 tablespoons tomato ketchup
4 tablespoons brown fruity sauce
1 teaspoon English mustard
1 tablespoon Worcestershire sauce
1 tablespoon brown sugar

Mix all the ingredients together in a small saucepan and bring to the boil, use hot or cold.

SPICED OIL

Use this delicious oil to brush over all barbecue meat and fish.

300m/1½ pt good quality light cooking oil, i.e.
   sunflower, soya or safflower oil
1 clove garlic
2 sprigs thyme
1 sprig rosemary
1 bay leaf
1 teaspoon mixed pickling spices
2 small dried chilli peppers

Place the oil in a screw-top bottle. Cut the garlic in half; add to the bottle with the herbs and spices. Seal and leave to infuse. Keeps for months.

SPICY BARBECUE SAUCE

A bit more preparation for this version, but it has a stronger kick!

25g/1oz butter
1 small onion, finely chopped
1 glove garlic, crushed
1 teaspoon chilli powder
1 teaspoon mustard powder
2 tablespoons black treacle
3 tablespoons vinegar
3 tablespoons Worcestershire sauce
2 tablespoons tomato purée
½ teaspoon Tabasco sauce
salt and pepper to taste

Melt the butter in a frying pan. Add the onion and garlic and fry for 2–3 minutes until soft. Add remaining ingredients with 150ml/¼ pint water and stir well. Bring to the boil, then simmer for 30 minutes.

CURRY SPICE SAUCE

A potent sauce to serve with barbecued sausages, chops or chicken.

4 cloves
2 teaspoons coriander seeds
1 teaspoon cumin seeds
½ teaspoon ginger
1 teaspoon turmeric
¼ teaspoon cinnamon
¼ teaspoon chilli powder
225g/8oz onions
2 cloves garlic
salt
6 tomatoes
2 tablespoons oil
2 tablespoons plain flour
1 chicken stock cube
1 teaspoon granulated sugar

Place cloves and coriander seeds in a basin; crush with the end of a rolling pin. Chop cumin seeds; add to basin with ginger, turmeric, cinnamon and chilli powder. Alternatively, blend in a liquidiser. Peel and slice onions. Crush garlic. Peel, deseed and chop tomatoes. Heat oil in a saucepan and fry spices for 2 minutes. Add onions and garlic; cook until soft—about 5 minutes. Stir in flour and tomatoes; cook for 2 minutes. Dissolve stock cube in ½ pint boiling water; add to sauce. Bring to boil; cover and simmer for 1 hour or until tomatoes are broken down and sauce is thick. Add sugar; taste and add more salt, if necessary.

SATÉ SAUCE

This is delicious spread over pork or chicken during the last few minutes or barbecueing, or served as an accompaniment to plain grilled food.

1 small onion, finely chopped
1 glove garlic, crushed
salt
4 tablespoons desiccated coconut
1 tablespoon oil
juice of ½ lemon
4 level tablespoons peanut butter
½ level teaspoon chilli powder
1 level teaspoon soft brown sugar
1 bay leaf

Place coconut in a jug and add 250ml/½ pint boiling water. Leave for 15 minutes, then strain in a sieve, reserving liquid, pressing until all liquid is removed from coconut. Heat oil in a saucepan. Add onion and garlic, and fry until onion is tender. Stir in coconut liquid, lemon juice, peanut butter, chilli powder, sugar and bay leaf. Bring to the boil, stirring; cover and simmer for 10–15 minutes, until sauce has thickened. Taste and add more salt if necessary. Remove bay leaf and serve sauce hot.

STARTERS & SALADS

HOUMUS
For 6 portions

This Middle Eastern dip is traditionally made with Tahini—a sesame seed paste. If you cannot find it, try to use sesame oil for a good flavour. Serve with strips of warm pitta bread.

two 396-g/14-oz cans chickpeas
2 cloves garlic, crushed
¼ teaspoon salt
6 tablespoons sesame oil or corn oil
4 tablespoons Tahini (optional)
2 tablespoons lemon juice

Drain chickpeas and press through a sieve with a wooden spoon. Add garlic to pea purée. Gradually beat in oil and lemon juice. Taste and add more salt or lemon juice as necessary. Beat in enough water (about 4 tablespoons) to give a soft dipping consistency. Alternatively, put chickpeas, peeled garlic, oil and lemon juice in a food processor and run machine until smooth. Gradually pour water through lid until the mixture gains a soft consistency. Store, covered, in refrigerator for up to 2 days.

TZATZIKI
4–6 portions

Cool and refreshing, this cucumber dip is best made with fresh mint, though dried mint also gives a good flavour. It's also delicious as a side dish with hot, spicy barbecue food.

450-g/15.9-oz carton natural yogurt
½ cucumber
¼ teaspoon salt
1 teaspoon chopped fresh mint (or ½ teaspoon dried mint)

Place a piece of kitchen paper in a sieve and drain yogurt through sieve for 1 hour. Finely dice the cucumber and stir into drained yogurt with the salt and mint. Leave flavours to mix for 1 hour before serving. Store, covered, in refrigerator for up to 2 days. Stir before serving.

TARAMASALATA
Serves 6

This is an ideal dip to serve as a starter while the barbecue gets going. Serve it with strips of pitta bread or crisp vegetables.

1 slice white bread
1 clove garlic, crushed
4 tablespoons lemon juice
100g/4oz smoked cods' roe
black pepper
150ml/¼ pint corn oil

Remove the crusts from the bread. Pour a little water over the bread, then squeeze out so that the bread is moist but not soaking. Cut cods' roe in half and scoop into a basin. Add bread, garlic, lemon juice and a little pepper. Beat with a wooden spoon until smooth. Gradually add the oil, beating well after each addition, until the mixture has the consistency of mayonnaise. Alternatively, blend ingredients in a food processor or liquidiser. Pour into a serving dish. Store (covered) in refrigerator for up to 2 days.

GREEN SALAD
Serves 10

A crisp green salad is always a fresh accompaniment to barbecued food. Add a can of drained artichoke hearts, chopped gherkins, or green olives for a change.

1 crisp lettuce
1 bunch watercress
1 cucumber
1 green pepper
3 tablespoons vegetable oil
1 tablespoon white wine winegar
pinch English mustard powder
salt and pepper

Trim lettuce and watercress, rinse and drain. Thinly slice cucumber. Slice pepper in rings, discarding core seeds and pith. Place together in a large serving dish. Shake oil, vinegar, mustard, salt and pepper together in a screw-topped jar. Pour dressing over and toss salad just before serving.

SPICED RICE
Serves 6

A good, nutty accompaniment to barbecue food, it's even nicer made with brown rice.

1 onion, peeled and finely chopped
1 tablespoon oil
1 teaspoon turmeric
2oz/50g mixed dried fruit
pinch of cayenne
2oz/50g flaked almonds
2oz/50g desiccated coconut
8oz/225g long-grain rice
2 tablespoons oil
1 tablespoon vinegar
2 tablespoons orange juice
salt and pepper

Fry the onion in the oil until transparent; add the turmeric, fruit, cayenne, almonds and coconut. Fry for another 2 minutes then allow to cool. Cook the rice in boiling salted water for 10–12 minutes or until tender. Drain. Add the onion mixture and stir well. Allow to cool. Mix together the oil, vinegar, orange juice and a good shake of salt and pepper and stir into rice. Serve cold.

WALDORF SALAD
Serves 10

A classic, crisp, fruity salad. Make it on the day, as it won't keep. Raisins make a nice addition, and if you prefer, substitute half of the mayonnaise with natural yogurt.

5 crisp dessert apples
2 tablespoons lemon juice
1 head celery, sliced
100g/4oz walnut pieces
8 tablespoons mayonnaise

Core the apples; cut into quarters and slice. Toss the apples in lemon juice. Place in a bowl with celery, walnuts and mayonnaise, mix well together and place in a serving dish.

SHREDDED SPRING SALAD

Serves 6–8 portions

This salad is so fresh and tasty it needs no salad dressing.

6 medium carrots
2 large leeks
4 spring onions
50g/2oz salted peanuts
a few crisp lettuce leaves to garnish

Peel and grate the carrots. Trim leeks, discarding tough green leaves. Slit leeks lengthways, rinse thoroughly, and slice thinly. Trim and finely slice the spring onions. Arrange lettuce leaves on a serving plate. Toss carrots, leeks, spring onions and peanuts together and pile on top of lettuce.
To make in advance: Toss salad together and store in a plastic bag in the base of refrigerator for up to 24 hours. Serve with lettuce.

POTATO SALAD

Serves 6

1kg/2lb potatoes
2 tablespoons cooking oil
1 tablespoon white wine vinegar
1 teaspoon coarse-grain mustard
salt and pepper
6 tablespoons mayonnaise
parsley, chives or spring onions, chopped

Cook the potatoes in boiling, salted water until tender. Drain and cube. Mix the oil, vinegar, mustard, salt and pepper together; pour over the warm potatoes and turn them until well coated. Leave to cool. Add mayonnaise and herbs and mix well together.

MAYONNAISE

1 egg yolk
½ teaspoon salt
¼ teaspoon dry mustard
¼ teaspoon caster sugar
300ml/½ pint salad oil
1 tablespoon vinegar or lemon juice

Place egg yolk, salt, mustard and sugar in a small basin; beat with a wooden spoon, whisk (or make in a liquidiser) until blended. Gradually add oil, beating well after each addition. When mixture begins to thicken, add oil, a teaspoonful at a time. When mixture becomes very thick, or when all the oil has been added, beat in vinegar or lemon juice.
Aioli: Blend two cloves of crushed garlic and 1 teaspoon of salt into the egg yolk before making.
Green Mayonnaise: Very finely chop a handful of fresh basil leaves or watercress and add to mayonnaise made with lemon juice rather than vinegar.
Tartare Sauce: Add 1 teaspoon finely grated onion, 1 tablespoon chopped capers, 2 chopped gherkins and 1 teaspoon chopped fresh parsley to the basic mayonnaise.
Seafood Sauce: Add 2 tablespoons tomato purée, 1 tablespoons lemon juice, 2 tablespoons medium-dry sherry, a few drops of Tabasco sauce (or a good pinch of cayenne) and a few drops of Worcestershire sauce to the mayonnaise. Serve over prawns or crabmeat.

THREE-BEAN SALAD
For 6 portions

Quick, filling and very tasty!

1 clove garlic (optional)
4 tablespoons corn oil
2 tablespoons vinegar
2 tablespoons lemon juice
1 teaspoon brown sugar
½ teaspoon mustard
2 tablespoons chopped fresh parsley
pepper
6 spring onions
396-g/14-oz can cannelini beans
425-g/15-oz can red kidney beans
425-g/15-oz can butter beans

Crush garlic, if used. Place in a mixing bowl with oil, vinegar, lemon juice, sugar, mustard, parsley and good shake of pepper. Beat together. Finely slice the spring onions; add to mixing bowl with drained beans, mix well, and turn in the dressing to coat.

CRACKED WHEAT SALAD
Serves 10

A Middle Eastern-style dish. Pre-cooked cracked wheat (Pourgouri) has a nutty flavour and simply needs soaking. Look for it in Continental stores and delicatessens. This salad can be made 2 days in advance.

250g/8oz pre-cooked cracked wheat
1 bunch spring onions
6 tomatoes
335-g/11.8-oz can Mexicorn
2 tablespoons chopped parsley
50g/2oz raisins
1 teaspoon chopped mint in vinegar
4 tablespoons olive or cooking oil
2 tablespoons wine or cider vinegar
½ teaspoon whole-grain mustard
salt and pepper

Soak the cracked wheat in cold water for 30 minutes. Drain well and leave on a clean tea towel to dry. Chop the spring onions; skin, deseed and chop the tomatoes. Drain the Mexicorn. Mix the wheat, onions, tomatoes and Mexicorn together with the parsley and raisins. Beat the remaining ingredients well together; pour over salad and toss until well coated. Season the salad well, and place in a serving dish.

HAVING A BARBECUE PARTY?

Do you ever feel on warm, sunny days that it would be fun to invite a few friends around for a casual evening's eating and entertainment? A barbecue is the ideal way to do just that. When everyone gathers around the barbecue, helps prepare the food and carry drinks and snacks, a barbecue is an entertainment in itself. It's a natural way to start conversation—conversation about food and eating!

An instant party can soon be put together for a few friends. A quick 'phone round to ask friends to bring sausages, burgers, steaks or chicken, bread, maybe a salad, some fruit or a bottle—and all you have to do is get out the barbecue and charcoal, make the sauces and all the extras. Together everyone contributes to the success of the evening.

Catering for a crowd needs a little more thought and preparation. How will you cope with the quantity of food? How will you cook and serve it all? What about china, cutlery or glass? Follow the suggestions below for helpful ideas.

1. Cheat as much as possible by pre-cooking sausages, burgers, or chicken pieces under the grill or in the oven. Then finish cooking them for a good few minutes over a hot barbecue so that you still get the smoky barbecue flavour and crisp coating.
2. Parboil potatoes in their skins so that jacket potatoes will take less time to cook, or bake in the oven until almost cooked; then place in hot coals for the last 15 minutes or so.
3. Warm garlic bread in the oven.
4. Pre-cook all sauces and keep warm on the barbecue grid.
5. Line plenty of roasting tins or trays with foil ready for cooking and carrying hot food.
6. Allow plenty of time for the barbecue coals to get really hot—at least 1 hour before you start cooking.
7. If you want the fire to keep going for a long time, make sure you have an edge of coals around the fire getting hot and ready to move into the centre. Cold coals will cool down the fire.
8. Consider the size and capacity of your barbecue. Ask friends to bring along their cookers too, or make an extra barbecue out of a suitable wheelbarrow. Alternatively, make a brick frame, and stand wire cooker racks between the bricks.
9. Order wine (five glasses from one 70cl bottle) or beer from an off-licence on a sale or return basis. Order glasses at the same time.
10. Use paper plates and plastic cutlery as much as possible or hire china and cutlery from catering companies. (Look in the yellow pages!)
11. Don't forget you'll need plenty of foil, paper towels, paper napkins and dustbin bags for rubbish!
12. It is important to provide good lighting if the party is to continue into late evening. Garden lighting kits are available from garden centres. Hurricane lamps can be hung from trees, or stick wax flares or outdoor candles in the garden.

INDEX